iPod® and MP3 Players

iPod® and MP3 Players

Stuart A. Kallen

LUCENT BOOKS
A part of Gale, Cengage Learning

GALE
CENGAGE Learning™

Detroit • New York • San Francisco • New Haven, Conn • Waterville, Maine • London

LIBRARY OF CONGRESS CATALOGING-IN-PUBLICATION DATA

Kallen, Stuart A., 1955-
    iPod and MP3 players / by Stuart A. Kallen.
        p. cm.--(Technology 360)
    Includes bibliographical references and index.
    ISBN 978-1-4205-0166-7 (hardcover)
    1. Digital music players--Juvenile literature. I. Title.
    ML74.K35 2010
    006.5--dc22

                        2010016850

Lucent Books
27500 Drake Rd
Farmington Hills MI 48331

ISBN-13: 978-1-4205-0166-7
ISBN-10: 1-4205-0166-6

Printed in the United States of America
1 2 3 4 5 6 7 14 13 12 11 10

Printed by Bang Printing, Brainerd, MN, 1st Ptg., 09/2010

CONTENTS

FOREWORD

As we go forward, I hope we're going to continue to use technology to make really big differences in how people live and work.
—Sergey Brin, cofounder of Google

The past few decades have seen some amazing advances in technology. Many of these changes have had a direct and measurable impact on the way people live, work, and play. Communication tools, such as cell phones, satellites, and the Internet, allow people to keep in constant contact across longer distances and from the most remote places. In fields related to medicine, existing technologies—digital imaging devices, robotics and lasers, for example—are being used to redefine surgical procedures and diagnostic techniques. As technology has become more complex, however, so have the related ethical, legal, and safety issues.

Psychologist B. F. Skinner once noted that "the real problem is not whether machines think but whether men do." Recent advances in technology have, in many cases, drastically changed the way people view the world around them. They can have a conversation with someone across the globe at lightning speed, access a huge universe of information with the click of a key, or become an avatar in a virtual world of their own making. While advances like these have been viewed as a great boon in some quarters, they have also opened the door to questions about whether or not the speed of technological advancement has come at an unspoken price. A closer examination of the evolution and use of these devices provides a deeper understanding of the social, cultural, and ethical implications that they may hold for our future.

The Lucent Books' Technology 360 series not only explores how evolving technologies work, but also examines the short- and long-term impact of their use on society as a whole. Each volume in Technology 360 focuses on a particular invention, device, or family of similar devices, exploring how the device was developed, how it works, its impact on society, and its possible future uses. Volumes also contain a chronology specific to each topic, a glossary of terms used in the text, and a subject index. Sidebars, photos and detailed illustrations, tables, charts and graphs help further illuminate the text.

Titles in this series feature inventions and devices familiar to most readers, such as robots, digital cameras, MP3 players, and video games. Not only will users get an easy-to-understand, "nuts and bolts" overview of these inventions, they will also learn just how much these devices have evolved. For example, in 1973 a Motorola cell phone weighed about 2 pounds (0.9kg) and cost four thousand dollars. Today cell phones weigh only a few ounces and are often inexpensive enough for every member of the family to have one. Lasers—long a staple of the industrial world—have become highly effective surgical tools, capable of reshaping the cornea of the eye and cleaning clogged arteries. Early video games were played on large machines in arcades; today games are played on sophisticated home systems that allow for multiple players and cross-location networking.

IMPORTANT DATES

1976 Electronics engineers Steve Jobs and Steve Wozniak form Apple, Inc. to develop desktop computers for the general public.

1999 Shawn Fanning makes his file-sharing software, Napster, available for free on the Internet.

1984
The first American CD, Bruce Springsteen's *Born in the USA*, goes on sale. This event introduces digital technology to the American public for the first time.

1994
The first MP3 encoder software program is released on the World Wide Web.

1985   1990   1995

1979
On July 1, Sony introduces the Walkman portable cassette player.

1997
Justin Frankel releases early digital jukebox software called WinAmp on the Internet.

in the Development of the iPod® and MP3 Players

2004
British reporter Ben Hammersley coins the term *podcasting*.

2007
Buyers stand in line for four days at Apple stores in major cities to be the first to purchase iPhones® when they go on sale.

2003 On April 28, Apple opens the iTunes Store, which sells over 1 million songs within the first five days of operation.

2006
Microsoft launches the Zune digital media player.

2000

2005

2010

2001
On October 23, Steve Jobs announces the creation of the iPod®.

2009
The Motorola Droid® is launched to compete with the iPhone.

2005
The iTunes Store begins offering music videos, TV shows, and podcasts.

A Rocking Revolution

In 1976 when Steve Jobs founded Apple Inc., he believed he could change the world by selling small personal computers. Although he was operating out of his parents' garage in Cupertino, California, Jobs envisioned Apple as a multibillion-dollar corporation. His dream came true in 1982 when Apple became the first personal computer company to reach $1 billion in annual sales. But Jobs is more than a computer geek. He also loves music and describes himself as an "obsessive Beatles fan."[1] Jobs had a vision of a day when music lovers would use their computers instead of records and cassette tapes to hear their favorite tunes. That dream came closer to reality in 1984 when the first American compact disc (CD), Bruce Springsteen's *Born in the USA*, went on sale.

CDs were the first music format to contain music coded as binary data, the language of computers. In the mid-1980s, personal computers did not have the memory or processing power to copy CDs. However, by the 1990s, computers were powerful enough to read and write the digital information stored on CDs. But when the first portable MP3 players were introduced in 1998, few people seemed interested in this new way to listen to music. Sales were slow for the MPMan and Rio PMP300, the first players sold in North America. Jobs wanted to know why. He took a hard look at the players available in stores and discovered that the devices were difficult to use because of their clunky operating systems. According to Jobs, there was "plenty of evidence from the MP3 players already out there that the consumer electronics makers don't know diddly about software."[2]

After making this observation, Jobs formed a team of computer wizards at Apple. They worked around the clock to devise an MP3 player that was so sleek, well crafted, and cutting edge that consumers would not be able to resist it. On October 23, 2001, Jobs felt he had succeeded. He stood on a stage at Apple and pulled a 6.4-ounce (28g) MP3 player out of the pocket of his jeans. He showed the small crowd of workers the first iPod® and announced that it was "a major, major breakthrough."[3]

iPod Nation

When Jobs introduced his major breakthrough, no one at Apple—or anywhere else—could have predicted that by October 2004, iPods would make up 90 percent of the MP3 player market. Even fewer would have believed that a portable music player could change society. In his book *The Perfect Thing*, author Steven Levy writes,

Steve Jobs, founder of Apple Computer Inc., introduces the company's first personal computer in 1977. Apple remains at the forefront of industry advances.

> No one envisioned subway cars and airplane cabins and street corners and school lounges and fitness centers where vast swaths of humanity would separate themselves from the bonds of reality via the White Earbud Express. No one expected that there would be magazine covers and front-page newspaper stories proclaiming [the United States] an "iPod Nation." . . . And certainly no one thought that the name of this tiny computer *cum* music player would became an appellation to describe an entire generation or a metaphor evoking any number of meanings: the future, great design, short attention span, or just plain coolness.[4]

Beyond its social implications, the iPod transformed the way the music industry distributed music. As the number of consumers using iPods exploded, the popularity of compact discs quickly fell. In 2008 consumers purchased about 500 million CDs, less than half the 1.2 billion CDs they bought in 2000.

Record Store Wreck

As the CD went the way of the cassette tape, traditional record stores suffered. While there were ninety-five hundred chain record stores in the United States in 1991, that number fell to around two thousand by 2009 with about one-third of the stores closing since 2003. These shops were once social institutions where consumers could gather with friends, hear new music, meet artists, and receive suggestion from knowledgeable store personnel.

Whatever the downside, brick-and-mortar record stores have been largely replaced by online music outlets, such as the iTunes Store, Amazon MP3, Zune Marketplace, and Rhapsody. And for those who wish to bypass paying for music entirely by illegally downloading copyrighted material, nearly every song ever recorded is available on peer-to-peer file-sharing applications, such as LimeWire and BitTorrent.

Blocking Yourself Off

In the first decade of the twenty-first century, iPods and similar players created a revolution by transforming the way people purchased and listened to music. But some see the iPod revolution as having negative consequences. Columnist Trey Treviño describes one social problem associated with iPods:

> With everyone walking around with their earbuds in, not only are people less likely to approach them, but they also give off the impression that they don't want to be approached. This, of course, leads to an overall decline in human interaction. . . . When you use your iPod constantly, you are, in effect, blocking yourself off from the world with music.[5]

A larger concern has been described by audiologists who say long exposure to loud music in earbud earphones is causing a type of hearing loss in young people formerly found only in older adults. Whatever the drawbacks, there is no stopping the iPod revolution. Future inventions might someday see the MP3 player go the way of the CD, but sales of MP3s and digital music players have helped companies in the burgeoning digital music industry reap billions of dollars in profits. For better or worse, the iPod nation continues to grow at a rapid rate with more than one out of every four Americans over the age of twelve listening to music on the digital devices. And the revolution has just begun.

CHAPTER 1

The Digital Media Explosion

Culture often changes dramatically when scientific discoveries can be connected to the arts. This was certainly the case when the transistor radio met rock and roll, a new form of music in the mid-1950s.

Transistors are small electronic devices that control the flow of electricity. Modern transistors are tiny, and billions of individual transistors are packed onto integrated circuits. Also known as microchips, these miniature electric circuits control nearly every computerized device from MP3 players to robots that build automobiles.

In 1955 transistors were huge by modern standards. But they allowed the production of small, handheld AM radios like the Regency TR-1, which measured 3 by 5 by 1.25 inches (7.6 cm by 12.7 cm by 3.2 cm). The radio came with a large gold tuning dial and, like modern MP3 players, it was available in a variety of colors, including pearl white, lavender, and lime. But the first radios were expensive. The Regency cost $50, equal to $325 in today's dollars. But over the years, prices dropped and by the late 1950s, Elvis Presley, Chuck Berry, Buddy Holly, and other rock singers were blasting out of tens of millions of transistor radios throughout the industrialized world.

Small, battery-operated transistor radios were the 1950s equivalent of MP3 players because they changed the way people listened to music. Rock and roll broadcast on AM radio was a new concept in the fifties, and the small portable radios were perfect for listening to this new format. They also allowed listeners, for the first time, to tune out the world by using earphones. In addition, radios created changes within the music industry by providing different standards for sound. This was especially true at the record label Motown, home of hit soul groups, like the Temptations, the Miracles, and the Supremes. Producers at Motown mixed the instrument and voice levels on songs using tiny transistor radio speakers. This was done so producers could hear the music the same way that teenagers heard it on their transistors at home.

Sony president Masaru Ibuka presents a number of the company's transistor radios in 1958. Transistor radios paved the way for today's MP3 players.

Like MP3 players, transistor radios made earlier listening devices, in this case large, boxy radios, nearly obsolete. But those who wanted to choose their own music had to listen to vinyl records that were anything but portable. Record players were big and heavy, and if they were bumped or jostled, their tone arms scratched across the vinyl. And the black vinyl records were easily damaged, leaving a listener to hear music through a loud series of pops, clicks, and skips.

The Walkman Decade

An alternative to the vinyl record first appeared in the mid-1960s. Engineers at the Dutch company Philips invented a portable tape recorder that worked with audio cassettes made with 0.13-inch (0.33cm) magnetic tape. The plastic tape is

HOW LOUD IS MY PLAYER?

Common Sounds	Thresholds	Average Decibels
	Threshold of hearing	0
Whisper		20
Refrigerator		40
Normal conversation		60
Rush hour traffic		80
	Level at which long exposure can cause hearing damage	85
Subway		90
Lawnmower		100
Rock concert		105
iPod® at top volume		115
	Threshold of pain	130
Fireworks		140
Commercial jet at take-off		140

Sound is measured in units called decibels (dB). Sounds that are extremely loud (120-150 dBs) or loud (85 dBs or more) for a long period of time can damage the inner ear, causing noise-induced hearing loss.

Because sounds above 85 decibels might not be physically painful but can still cause hearing damage, experts suggest listening at 60 percent of the maximum volume on portable music players.

coated with a magnetic iron substance called ferric oxide, which stores sound as a series of electronic signals. When the tape passes over a playback head in a tape recorder, sound is reproduced through a speaker.

Philips marketed the cassette recorder to reporters who could use the small machines to record interviews. They were also sold to executives who used them to record letters for secretaries to type up at a later date.

As early as 1965, a few record companies released albums on cassettes. These could be played on the popular cassette deck Philips sold under the brand name Norelco Carry-Corder. This machine was a monophonic (nonstereo) device that ran on five D batteries and weighed over 3 pounds (1.4kg). However, early cassettes were low fidelity and did not reproduce the full range of music heard on vinyl records. Cassettes also had a notable hiss, prompting music critics to deride them as toys for children, not carriers of music for sophisticated ears.

Criticism of cassettes largely ended in 1971 with the introduction of tapes coated with a synthetic magnetic substance called chromium dioxide. Another development, a recording system called Dolby B, helped reduce tape hiss. When used together, Dolby B and chromium dioxide tape extended the frequency range of cassettes and introduced the era of high-fidelity, portable music. Interest in cassettes continued to grow with the introduction of the Sony Walkman in Japan on July 1, 1979. This portable, battery-operated, blue-and-white tape deck weighed 0.9 pound (0.4kg) and was operated by buttons which allowed listeners to play, fast forward, and rewind the tapes. The device had no external speaker but users were able to hear their music through lightweight headphones.

Sony did not expect to create a sensation. When the company first introduced the Walkman, it expected to sell about five thousand machines a year. However, Sony sold more than fifty thousand Walkmans in two months. And the device was nearly as expensive as an iPod Classic, selling for the equivalent of $275. However, prices fell when cheaper imitations were marketed by Aiwa, Panasonic, and Toshiba. By 1983, music cassettes were outselling vinyl records, and three years later, the word *Walkman*, used to describe any cassette player, entered the *Oxford English Dictionary*.

Sony introduced the Walkman, a portable cassette player, and they quickly became a success with consumers.

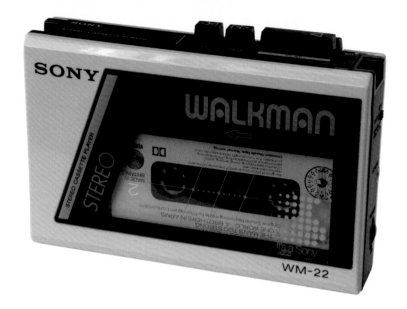

"Home Taping Is Killing Music"

Cassette players ushered in a new kind of music revolution. In addition to portable Walkmans, high-quality cassette decks, which plugged into home stereo systems, grew in popularity. By the late 1970s for the first time, music lovers could create "mix tapes" at home with their favorite songs and listen to them on the go with their Walkmans. The introduction of cassette players in cars also helped increase demand for home cassette recorders. Record company executives, however, were not happy with this development.

In the early 1980s the British Phonographic Industry (BPI), an industry trade group, took out full-page ads in magazines with the headline, "Home taping is killing music."[6] The ads featured a drawing of a cassette as a skull, perched above crossbones. The cassette portrayed as a pirate flag was part of an anti-taping ad campaign. It was initiated by record company executives who believed that people were using cassettes to tape their friends' records rather than buying new ones.

However, cassette taping did not damage the music industry as some feared. In fact, by 1983, prerecorded cassettes were outselling vinyl records for the first time. By the end of the eighties, over 500 million prerecorded cassettes were sold annually in the United States alone.

The "High-Tech Wonder" of CDs

Cassette sales started to decline with the rise of another new media, the compact disc (CD). Although the CD was invented in 1965 by physicist James Russell, discs did not become popular until 1984 when rock superstars, such as Billy Joel and Bruce Springsteen, began releasing their albums on disc.

Unlike cassettes, in which sound is reproduced by electronic signals on the magnetic surface of a tape, CDs contain digital information. When music is recorded digitally, the sound is converted to the binary code which is the language of all computers. Digital information provides a much more accurate replication of sound and can be easily transferred to a computer or other digital device. The general public was not aware of the technological advantages of digital discs. Most only knew that CDs sounded much better than cassettes and vinyl records.

In 1984 consumer interest in CDs increased dramatically when Sony introduced the CD version of the Walkman

A radio disc jockey loads a CD into a player while, at right, a vinyl record sits in a player. The digital information on CDs allowed for better sound replication than cassettes and led to fewer cassette and record sales.

called the Discman. (The name Discman was changed to CD Walkman in 1998.) By 1985 CDs were selling so quickly some retailers could not keep them on their store shelves and *Time* magazine was referring to the CD as a "high-tech wonder."[7] CD players for homes and cars became the fastest-selling machines in consumer electronics history.

Music for Free

Although CDs were popular, they cost about 50 percent more than cassettes and records, so music fans continued to purchase older technology. Thirty-five million CD players were purchased worldwide in 1990, compared to 180 million cassette machines. In addition, cassettes continued to outsell CDs two to one with 1.4 billion cassettes purchased compared to 700 million CDs. Records also remained in the mix, with 339 million sold that year.

While consumers were purchasing record players, cassette decks, and CDs players, computers played almost no role in music reproduction. That is because during this era computer hard drives were so small they could not even hold a single song. For example, the state-of-the-art Macintosh Classic, introduced in 1990, had a 4-megabyte (MB) hard drive. A file containing a single, four-minute song on a CD was ten times larger, about 40 megabytes. However, that same year, the company that popularized the cassette deck introduced new technology that would someday lead to a boom in CD reproduction.

In 1990 Philips marketed the first CD-R (compact disc-recordable). This was the first recordable CD, and it could hold 650 megabytes of information, or about sixteen, four-minute songs. However, the machines used to record CD-Rs, called rewriters, were not meant for average consumers. A rewriter was the size of a washing machine and cost thirty-five thousand dollars. This meant recordable CDs were not a threat to the music industry—yet.

However, the trade group Recording Industry Association of America (RIAA) was worried about another digital system. One of the missions of the RIAA was stopping music

bootleggers and counterfeiters who profited by releasing unauthorized CDs, vinyl records, and cassettes. Therefore the RIAA was alarmed in the late 1980s, when Sony announced the launch of the Digital Audio Tape (DAT) system. Digital Audio Tape is similar to a CD in that it plays sound files in digital form. However, unlike cassettes with their inferior sound, DAT machines make perfect reproductions of CDs using the digital binary language of computers.

Executives of the Recording Industry Association of America speak out against music bootlegging at a 2005 news conference.

The RIAA went to court and prevented the sale of DAT machines in the United States. After successfully stopping Sony, record industry executives lobbied Congress to pass the Audio Home Recording Act of 1992. The law required DAT machines to contain a microchip that would prevent users from making more than one, single copy of a CD. With this requirement, according EMI Records executive Joe Smith, "we killed the DAT machine."[8]

While the Audio Home Recording Act might have killed the DAT machine, the law did not cover CD-R recorders, called rewrite drives. By this time, technological advances were allowing computer makers to produce rewrite drives that were small and inexpensive. Although the RIAA was strongly opposed to the idea, the Audio Home Recording Act allowed computers to be sold with built-in CD rewrite drives. The law also exempted computer makers from installing microchips that would limit the number of copies users could make. This was a big win for the computer industry, and by the second half of the 1990s, the consequences of the rewrite drive loophole in the law were apparent. As Steve Gottlieb, owner of TVT Records, explains, "you could have all the music you want for free."[9]

Part of the reason CD-Rs were so popular had to do with the fact that record companies were selling CDs by hit recording artists for an all-time high of $18.98 each, equivalent to $30 today. Those who wished to avoid paying such high prices could borrow a prerecorded CD from a friend—or

"Two Words: *Ripping* and *Burning*"

In his book *Appetite for Self-Destruction* music journalist Steve Knopper describes how CD rewrite drives on computers harmed one record store owner:

In 1994, Andy Schneidkraut, owner of Albums on the Hill, a twenty-year-old record store at . . . the University of Colorado in Boulder, had his best year ever. He sold 1,800 copies of the Dave Matthews Band's *Under the Table and Dreaming* CD to legions of college students. Life was good. But his exuberance was short-lived. By the end of the 1990s, he was lucky to sell 200 copies of *any* record. Why? Two words: *ripping* and *burning*. CU students began to show up on campus with

their own PCs, all equipped with the CD-rewrite drives. . . . No longer did every Dave Matthews Band fan drop by Albums for a $16.99 CD. *One* fan would drop by for the CD and burn copies for the other fifty kids on his dorm hall. . . . "It was like a knife in my back—if someone would come up and say, 'I'd like the new Dave Matthews, and can I get twenty-five blank CDs please?'" says Schneidkraut . . . [whose] annual revenues have dropped from $600,000 [in 1992] to $240,000 [in 2008].

Steve Knopper, *Appetite for Self-Destruction*, New York: Free Press, 2009, pp. 78–79.

checkout a copy from a library—and copy it. CD-Rs cost $6 to $10 each in 1998 ($8 to $13 today). A 1998 article in *Time* magazine reports, "There's [a] wild card in the audio deck: computers. CD recorders for PCs cost as little as $300, and the Internet, to which more and more PCs are attached, is emerging as a hothouse for new music."[10]

A New Generation of Music Pirates

By 1998 the RIAA was starting to understand that CD-Rs were threatening the music business. Spokesperson Cary Sherman stated: "Recordable CDs have become the tool of choice for a new generation of music pirates."[11] However, even as the RIAA spoke out against CD-Rs, a new music format was gaining popularity: MP3. And the MP3 would quickly make recordable CDs a minor problem for the recording industry.

The MP3 is a digital coding and compression technology that reduces the size of CD music files to one-twelfth of their original size. The format was painstakingly developed over the course of twelve years in Germany by audio engineer Karlheinz Brandenburg. On July 7, 1994, the Fraunhofer Society, a group made up of German engineers and scientists, released the first MP3 encoder software program on the World Wide Web. In 1994 the Web was not quite three years old, but nineteen-year-old music lover Justin Frankel from Sedona, Arizona, understood the implications of the new technology and began work on an MP3 player, also called a jukebox, after the machine that plays a wide variety of songs.

Although Frankel was a college dropout, he was a computer genius. He set up a software company called Nullsoft and produced a keystroke logging program while still in high school. On April 21, 1997, Frankel released the MP3 digital jukebox WinAmp on the Internet. WinAmp was free but Frankel asked users to send a ten-dollar donation. By 1998 more than 15 million people had downloaded the program and Frankel

Bits & Bytes

$59 million

Amount AOL paid college dropout Justin Frankel in 1999 for the WinAmp MP3 software jukebox he invented while living with his parents was earning more than $100,000 a year. He sold his company to America Online (AOL) the following year and made a profit of $59 million.

A Million Hits a Day

WinAmp stimulated widespread interest in MP3 music files. Seven months after the software was released, computer entrepreneur Michael Robertson took advantage of that interest, founding the Web site MP3.com. Robertson got the idea for the company after viewing logs on a search engine he ran called Filez, which was popular in the days before Google. One day he noticed that many thousands of people were searching for MP3s, a term that was unfamiliar to him. Robertson later said, "I didn't know what that was, but I thought if people are searching for it, it must be an opportunity."[12]

MP3 Technology

In the twenty-first century, millions of MP3 files are transmitted over the Internet every day. But the file format that made iPods and other MP3 players so popular was invented long before most people ever heard of the Internet. In 1979 Karlheinz Brandenburg, a German audio engineer in Erlangen, was trying to find a way to better transmit speech over phone lines. Brandenburg assembled a team of fifteen researchers to expand their understanding of the little-known science of audio compression. The team worked for years, meticulously entering complex formulas on primitive computers to analyze sound. Rather than use voice files, the team dissected the Suzanne Vega song "Tom's Diner," in which she sings a cappella (without musical instruments). Twelve years after Brandenburg started his work, he was able to compress "Tom's Diner" into a format called ISO-MPEG-1 Audio Layer 3, or MP3. Brandenburg played the song on a computer with a software program he developed. Dozens of others worked on perfecting the MP3 format over the years including researchers in the United States and the Netherlands. Brandenburg became known as the father of the MP3 in the late 1990s, when millions of computer users began downloading and trading MP3s. Because her song was used during the research, Vega is jokingly referred as the mother of the MP3.

Robertson did some research and listened to an MP3 of "Take Five," a classic song by legendary jazz pianist, Dave Brubeck. He was amazed that his computer was able to perform the same functions as his stereo. In order to direct people searching for MP3s to Filez, Robertson set up MP3.com. The first day, while the home page was still blank, MP3.com received over eighteen thousand unique users.

In the weeks that followed, Robertson asked independent musicians and unsigned bands if they wanted to store their songs and promote their music for free on MP3.com. In exchange, the bands would give Robertson a few tracks to use for free. Although music industry analysts thought Robertson was crazy to give away music, the site thrived and accumulated over a million songs from 150,000 bands. The site also attracted intense interest from listeners and received over a million visitors a day.

MP3.com also attracted investors and in July 21, 1999, the site announced an initial public offering (IPO). An IPO is a financial process where a company makes stock available to the public for the first time. Within days, Robertson raised a record-setting $370 million.

"It's Not Just a Phase"

The great enthusiasm over MP3.com soon faded when record companies discovered the site. They learned that MP3.com had purchased forty-five thousand recorded CDs by various artists and made them available for free downloading. This violated copyright laws. A copyright gives artists, publishers, and record companies the right to control the use and reproduction of original works. Giving away thousands of copies of a song without the permission of the copyright holder is an act of copyright infringement and is illegal. Anyone who is found guilty of violating copyright laws must pay the copyright holder for use of the material. When thousands of people download a single song, the copyright holder may be entitled to tens of thousands of dollars.

The RIAA sued MP3.com for $150,000 for each CD it made available on the site. Robertson responded by saying he had data that proved his system was making money for record companies since it encouraged people to listen to and

Musician Tom Petty meets with fans in Hollywood after the release of his album Echo *in 1999. Petty allowed a song from the album to be downloaded for free on MP3.com to better reach his fans and encourage album sales.*

buy more music. One example that supported Robertson's case concerned Tom Petty's hard-hitting single "Free Girl Now." In March 1999 Petty uploaded a free version of the song to MP3.com and within three days more than 150,000 fans downloaded the single. Each downloader was required to provide an e-mail address and other information. Petty was able to use the e-mail addresses to promote his new album *Echo*, which includes "Free Girl Now." The album became a best seller and those who downloaded the song were also notified about Petty's 1999 summer tour, which eventually brought in $27 million.

Despite Petty's success, his record company, Warner Bros., which owned part of the copyright on "Free Girl Now" ordered MP3.com to stop the free downloads. Petty understood why Warner Bros. was upset but he says, "I thought this is what would happen anyway eventually with music, so let's get [record companies] used to it. The industry is probably going to have to do a lot with the Internet in the next few years. It's not just a phase."[13]

Whatever Petty's belief, the RIAA prevailed in its lawsuit against MP3.com. The judge in the case ruled that Robertson was violating copyrights laws. He was forced to pay record companies $200 million and MP3.com was eventually shut down.

The Napster Boom

While the RIAA was satisfied that it had destroyed a threat to record company profits, the destruction of MP3.com had unforeseen consequences that shook the industry to its roots. Robertson had been eager to work with record companies to promote music and help them profit by charging small fees for each song. Instead, with MP3.com bankrupted, people searching for songs online soon learned about a new technology called peer-to-peer (P2P) file sharing.

P2P gained popularity when Shawn Fanning, an eighteen-year-old student at Northeast University in Boston, Massachusetts, invented a software program called Napster. Fanning was interested in sharing his MP3 music files with his friends, so he spent a few weeks writing lines of computer code on his laptop. The resulting computer program allowed P2P sharing through high-speed Internet connections. (At the time, most people connected to the Internet through telephone modems that transferred information at a much slower rate, but many people were upgrading to broadband connections, which allows much faster downloads.)

To employ Napster, a user simply typed the name of a song into a search box. The program then scanned computer hard drives of anyone else who had downloaded Napster. Within seconds, the software located song files, cataloged their titles and the albums on which they appeared, and indexed the bands

Shawn Fanning founded Napster, a popular software program that allowed for the sharing of MP3 music files until it was shut down by court order.

that performed the songs. Users could then use Napster to download the songs.

After Fanning made Napster available online in June 1999, the program went viral, that is, it rapidly spread from person to person over the Internet. Once again, the music industry reacted with a lawsuit. In December 1999 the RIAA sued Fanning for about $20 million, charging that "nearly every hit song by every significant recording artist can be found on Napster."[14] Rather than stop file sharing, the publicity surrounding the case spurred intense interest in Napster. Within a month, the number of users tripled to 150,000, and Napster's catalog of songs quadrupled to 20 million. By early 2001 the number of Napster users exploded to more than 30 million. Forty percent of the users were college students in the United States, and 2.8 billion files per month were being downloaded worldwide.

Nearly every work of music that had ever been recorded on a CD was available on Napster. In addition, the site was a music lover's paradise, filled with obscure files never released by record companies. These included bootleg albums, outtakes, alternate versions of songs, and live concerts taped by audience members.

Even as the number of users increased daily, the Ninth Circuit Court of Appeals ordered Napster to remove all copyrighted material from its site in February 2001. Rather than do so, Fanning tried to bargain with the record companies. He offered to turn Napster into a subscription service in which users would pay about $10 a month to download songs. The record companies would receive over $200 million per year in the deal. However, the record companies refused, believing this new method of music distribution was a major threat to profits. Napster shut down in July 2001 and declared bankruptcy in 2002.

An Exciting New Development

Before Napster was invented, a handful of powerful corporations kept tight control over all music and profited from sales of every song and album. After Napster was introduced, CD sales began to decline practically overnight.

Becoming a Software Developer

Job Description: Software developers test and verify existing software, design new software, manage projects, and consult with computer companies about software design.

Education: A bachelor's degree in computer science.

Qualifications: In this competitive field, qualified software developers must be familiar with programming languages such as Perl, PHP, Java, ColdFusion, and ASP. In addition, qualified developers often create their own free "shareware" software applications which make them more desirable to employers.

Additional Information: While stories about college dropouts earning millions in software design are common, it is difficult to get a job as a software engineer without a four year degree.

Salary: $55,000 to $68,000 per year

Because of well-established copyright laws, downloading music without paying for it is illegal. While this might be the case, music lovers will always find ways to share songs whether they are reproduced on the magnetic tapes, CD-Rs, or digital computer files. This reflects the power of music, which some say was invented by prehistoric humans even before the spoken word. And technology has only helped to perpetuate the love of song. As the record companies discovered, it is difficult to exercise rigid control over something as universally powerful and desirable as music.

Music forms a personal bond between listener and performer, and that connection cannot always be bought or sold. While the industry managed to capitalize on that bond, the digital language of computers unleashed a new concept that is as ancient as primitive cave dwellers singing around a campfire. Music can be free to those who want it. On his Web site in 2001 recording artist Prince writes, "from the point of view of a real music lover, [Napster] can only be viewed as an exciting new development in the history of music."[15]

CHAPTER 2

Portable Digital Players

In early 1998 Bill Kincaid was driving on a freeway in northern California. He was planning to spend the day practicing behind the wheel of his Formula Ford at a racetrack in Willows. Kincaid was more than a race-car driver, however. He had spent the early 1990s working on an important operating system upgrade for Apple Inc. The system was never put to use, and Kincaid quit his job at Apple. But as the software engineer was driving, he heard a news report on the radio that caught his attention. He said, "Somebody was talking about the latest geek toy, a little device called a Rio that was like a . . . Walkman that played something called MP3 files (first I'd ever heard of them)."[16]

Kincaid was riveted, but at the end of the story the announcer stated that Mac (Macintosh) users should not get too excited. The Rio PMP300, one of the first commercially available MP3 players, did not work with Macintosh computers. Kincaid, a software wizard, thought to himself "Ha! I can fix *that*!"[17] The next day Kincaid called Diamond Multimedia, the company that sold the Rio. He convinced Diamond Multimedia to let him write a program that would make the Rio compatible with Macs. Kincaid then recruited his friend Jeff Robbins, another computer genius who had once worked at Apple, to help him with the task.

A Digital Jukebox

The Rio PMP300 was about the size of a deck of cards and could hold about twenty-four MP3s. With its big, round dial, used for skipping tracks forward or backward, it resembled an early transistor radio. However, the player also had thoroughly modern features, such as the small liquid crystal display (LCD) screen and four preset equalizer settings, to adjust sound quality. The MP3 player did have several drawbacks. Consumers complained the operating system was difficult to use and the screen did not display artists or song information. Kincaid and Robbins felt they could create a vastly improved operating system for the Rio. They went to work in their living rooms, spending days learning everything they could about MP3s and the complex math, source codes, and industry standards behind the format. Commenting on this period, Kincaid says, "Wow. What an experience. Every day it felt like my head would explode."[18] Despite the difficulties of the task, by the summer of 1999, the two computer wizards completed a piece of software, a digital audio program called SoundJam MP. SoundJam was much more than a way for the Rio to interface, or work with, Mac computers. The program also had many

Digital music players, from left, the RioRiot, iPod, and Nomad Jukebox 3, were among the first devices to provide clear quality playback of MP3 files.

advanced features. The digital audio software had dedicated bass, treble, and balance controls, a ten-band graphic equalizer, the ability to randomly shuffle songs, a visualizer that showed colorful random effects, and a display that showed all the songs available, the artists, and albums. According to author Steven Levy, these features, which were previously lacking on the Rio operating system, meant SoundJam "was a full-featured digital jukebox that even had hippy-dippy light shows that filled the screen while you played your songs."[19]

Digital Audio to the Masses

Around the time the Rio was released with Mac-compatible SoundJam software, Apple's chief executive officer, Steve Jobs, began to worry that his company might have waited too long to develop an MP3 player. He realized that Diamond Multimedia had beaten Apple to the market with a sophisticated MP3 player, a new type of technology that could be used with his company's computers. Time was of the essence. Rather than put current Apple programmers to work designing a unique MP3 jukebox, he called Kincaid and Robbins. Jobs told them he wanted to purchase SoundJam, so it could be bundled (provided free) with the Macintosh operating system. However, Jobs felt SoundJam needed to be improved before it could be branded with the Apple logo. Robbins says, "Apple takes complicated concepts and makes [them] just incredibly simple and easy to use."[20]

Within four months, SoundJam was redesigned and renamed iTunes. On January 9, 2001, Jobs demonstrated the digital jukebox software to Macintosh enthusiasts at the Macworld Conference & Expo in San Francisco, California. The brilliantly user-friendly iTunes was a hit with the industry insiders at the expo, but its use was limited. While iTunes worked with any MP3 player available at the time, few people owned such devices. According to Apple vice president Greg Joswiak, "the products stank."[21] People tended to buy players like the Rio and become frustrated because they could only

hold twenty-four songs, and the controls were difficult to use, which made browsing through even a limited number of songs difficult. Joswiak says most MP3 owners had the same story: "'I got it, it was cute, and now it's in the drawer.' That means no telling your friends how cool it is. Because it isn't cool."[22] Jobs planned to change all that.

In January 2001 Apple's senior vice president of hardware, Jon Rubenstein, assured Jobs he could create an MP3 player that could hold hundreds, or even thousands, of songs. And it would be smaller than a deck of cards. But Jobs had another demand. The product would have to be ready in time for the Christmas shopping season, little more than ten months away. In order to meet this seemingly impossible deadline, Rubenstein called on Tony Fadell, a thirty-two-year-old engineer who was a renowned expert on digital audio and MP3 technology. After Rubenstein explained what Jobs wanted, Fadell said, "This is the project that's going to remold Apple and 10 years from now, it's going to be a music business, not a computer business."[23]

In 2001, Macintosh introduced iTunes, a program that worked with any MP3 device to play music. The program initially faced the challenge that MP3 players were not yet very popular with the public.

Three Pushes of a Button

Fadell was aware of a new, compact MP3 player under development by a company called PortalPlayer in nearby Santa Clara. However, the device was considered ugly and clunky, like an FM radio with a set of large buttons protruding from the case. On the other hand, Macintosh computers were famous for their exceptional, sleek appearance. Despite PortalPlayer's design flaws, Fadell believed its hardware could be reengineered to fit inside a beautifully designed case compatible with Apple's distinct line of products.

Apple made a deal to work with PortalPlayer to develop an MP3 player. In the eight months that followed a team of 280 programmers, designers, and hardware engineers worked around the clock. Their goal was to build an MP3 player that would be irresistible to the masses and connect billions of people to digital music through Apple products and services. According to PortalPlayer senior manager Ben Knauss, "Tony's [Fadell's] idea was to take an MP3 player, build a Napster music sale service to complement it, and build a company around it. Tony had the business idea."[24]

While Fadell might have come up with the original business concept, Jobs was involved with every aspect of the design. Knauss recalls,

> They'd have meetings and Steve would be horribly offended he couldn't get to the song he wanted in less than three pushes of a button. We'd get orders: "Steve doesn't think it's loud enough, the sharps aren't sharp enough, or the menu's not coming up fast enough." Every day there were comments from Steve saying where it needed to be.[25]

In the months that followed, several prototypes were designed and rejected. However, on October 23, Jobs held a news conference to announce the release of the Apple iPod, an MP3 player with an unprecedented 5-gigabyte (GB) storage capacity, enough to hold roughly one thousand songs. Jobs, using his typical over-the-top promotional skills, called the new iPod, "insanely great."[26]

Unlike most electronics, the iPod had been designed from the outside in, with the smooth, compact case reflecting the

Inside Hard Drives and Flash Drives

The iPod could not exist were it not for the tiny hard drive that stores thousands of songs, videos, movies, and other files. These hard drives, which weigh about 1.7 ounces (48g) are technological wonders. Until 1980, hard drives consisted of 14-inch (35.6cm) platters that were housed in cases the size of washing machines. A 26-megabyte drive of this type, with storage space similar to a second-generation iPod, cost more than ten thousand dollars. However, hard drives began to shrink in the 1980s and the smaller digital storage devices made desktop and laptop personal computers possible. The 1.8-inch (4.6cm) hard drive in classic iPods was invented in 1993.

And the urge to shrink continues. In 2004 the 0.85-inch (2cm) Toshiba hard drive with an 8GB storage capacity entered the *Guinness Book of World Records* book for the smallest hard disk drive.

Despite their small size, many MP3 players, such as the iPod Shuffle, do not use hard drives. Instead they rely on flash memory, inexpensive digital devices that store information. Flash memory players cannot hold as many songs as those with hard drives. But they are smaller, use less battery power, and are resistant to shock. MP3 players with flash memory can be severely shaken while the user is running or exercising without fear that the motion will cause a song to skip.

Many MP3 players use tiny flash drives such as those shown here. They are small, inexpensive, and can store a lot of information.

classic Apple elegance. The components inside the device had to be extremely compact, and therefore advanced, to fit inside the sleek outer shell. For example, the Toshiba hard drive was the smallest available at time, measuring only 1.8-inches (4.6cm) across. While the Toshiba drive,

BITS & BYTES

125,000

Number of iPods sold within ten weeks of its initial October 2001 commercial release

technically known as a hard disk drive, was tiny, it performed the functions of much larger drives found in every computer. That is, it stored digital information, in this case song files, application software, and an operating system.

The iPod's hard drive was layered into the small case with other units, including a rechargeable Sony lithium battery and a microchip from PortalPlayer that controlled the functions of the player. These essential elements were packed together with a scroll wheel and a small LCD screen that displayed songs, albums, and artists. The scroll wheel physically rotated, allowing users to select "Play," "Menu," "Next," and "Previous" and to access music, contacts, and device settings. The battery provided about ten hours of listening enjoyment on a single charge.

The iPod ran iTunes software and could be plugged into any Apple computer through the Firewire port (also called the IEEE 1394 interface). Firewire, a method of transferring data at high speeds, was invented by Apple in 1995 and was a standard feature on all first-generation iPods. When the device was plugged into a computer, the songs stored on the hard drive would automatically download onto the iPod. While few understood the technical aspects of Apple's MP3 player, Jobs declared, "With iPod, listening to music will never be the same again."[27] The public was quick to agree. Between October 23, 2001, and January 1, 2002, over 125,000 iPods were sold for $399 apiece.

iPod Evolution

While Apple managed to rush the iPod to market before Christmas 2001, the company already had plans to introduce more advanced models. In March 2002 a 10GB iPod was introduced for $499.

The new iPods were popular with people who owned Macintosh computers. However, iPods and iTunes were designed to work only with Macintosh operating systems. That meant the iPod was not compatible with 95 percent of all computers, PCs that ran the Windows operating systems. That problem was solved in October 2002 when the second-generation PC-compatible iPod was released, bundled with a Windows-based software program called Music-Match Jukebox.

The most-advanced, second-generation iPods featured 20-gigabyte hard drives. They also came with a feature that made iPods unique at the time. The devices were controlled with a touch wheel. The stationary touch-sensitive ring allowed users to control the iPod functions by sliding their fingers around the wheel. This was advantageous because the single control let users navigate song lists, adjust volume, and select "Play," "Pause," "Forward," and "Reverse."

With the futuristic touch pad and the ability to hold up to four thousand songs, the new iPods quickly became the fastest growing fad of the twenty-first century. Several other MP3 players were launched to compete with the iPod, but the public did not embrace them. For example, SonicBlue, having acquired Diamond Multimedia in 1999, introduced the 20GB RioRiot in 2002. But critics complained that the RioRiot was as large as a paperback book, the controls were clunky, and software was difficult to navigate. Because it lacked a Firewire plug, the RioRiot took sixteen hours to fully load, compared with about two minutes for an iPod. Because of its shortcomings, RioRiots were only among 10 percent of MP3 players sold in 2002, while the iPod dominated with two-thirds of all sales.

Competition was also neutralized by brilliant marketing by Apple. The company sold limited editions with the engraved signatures of pop icons, including singers Beck and Madonna and skateboard legend Tony Hawk. The cult of the iPod continued to grow in April 2003 when the iTunes Store opened. This online music store sold MP3s for $0.99 per song and $9.99 per album.

The iPod became a runaway success in the twenty-first century. Apple came to produce several designs, from left, the iPod Shuffle, iPod Nano, and iPod Classic.

The third-generation iPod, introduced in September 2003, was thinner than its predecessors. The bulky Firewire port was replaced with a dock connector, a thirty-pin plug that connected the iPod to a common USB port found on all computers. Since most PCs did not have Firewire ports, the dock connector allowed Windows users to easily connect the iPod to their computers. With more PC users purchasing the device, Apple announced it had sold its one millionth iPod in October 2003. Three months later that number had doubled to 2 million iPods sold.

By 2004 the sleek, stylish, third-generation iPod had become a cultural touchstone. The miniaturized technology allowed a user to hold an entire music library in the palm of the hand and tune out the world for hours at a time. One

iPod Paraphernalia

The immense popularity of iPods did more than boost Apple's profit margins. An entire market developed to provide accessories to iPod users. By 2006 over two thousand products were available, including cases, speakers, earphones, armbands, docking stations, and converters for automobiles. At that time, for every $3 spent on an iPod, $1 was spent on accessories, creating an $850 million market in iPod paraphernalia. Accessories included a baby stroller with speakers, an iPod dock, and a massage chair with an iPod holder in the armrest. Even auto manufacturers could not ignore the iPod craze. By 2009 over 90 percent of all cars sold in the United States had the option for iPod connectivity. General Motors cars were sold with the PAL (personal audio link) that allowed users to play iPods through the vehicle's audio system. Those with more expensive tastes could purchase a $267,000 Bentley Continental with an iPod connectivity kit. This allowed drivers to work their iPods with controls mounted on the steering wheel. To ensure nothing happened to the iPod, it was stored in a fleece lined leather holder, safely located in the glove compartment.

unnamed New York user wrote enthusiastically about his iPod in an online survey conducted in February 2004:

> The design is just flawless. It feels good, to hold it in your hand, to rub your thumb over the navigation wheel and to touch the smooth white surface. It looks nice, I'm proud of owning such a device. It represents and holds an important part of my life, so I don't want an "ugly" package around it. I have never cherished anything I bought as much as this little device. When I was a child, I used to watch a kids' show called *The Music Machine* and I always dreamed of having something like that. A device that plays any song there is. The iPod comes pretty close to the fulfillment of this childhood fantasy.[28]

Music Goes Mini

Apple continued to attract new fans and make headlines when Jobs introduced the iPod Mini at the Macworld Conference & Expo in January 2004. The player was constructed with a new generation of tiny hard drives. And it truly was mini; the player was half an inch thick and the size of a business card, about 3.6 by 2 inches (9cm by 5cm). The 3.6 ounce (102g) player had 4-gigabyte memory, which held as many songs as the first-generation iPod introduced three years earlier. The Mini contained another advanced piece of technology, a touch pad called a click wheel. Different from the third-generation iPod, there were no function buttons above the touch pad wheel. Users could select "Play," "Menu," and other functions by clicking mechanical buttons located under the circular touch pad. Minis were also colorful. The white case was replaced with an eye-catching array of silver, blue, green, pink, or gold.

The Mini was priced at $249, only $50 less than the 15-gigabyte, third-generation iPod. Some complained about the price, lending credibility to critics who said iPod stood for "Idiots Price Our Devices."[29] However, when it was announced that the Mini would go on sale February 20, Apple received over one hundred thousand preorders. And days before the Mini appeared in stores, iPod fanatics began lining up in front of retailers, camping out in line. When the

Apple CEO Steve Jobs, right, and musician John Mayer examine an iPod Mini during the 2004 Macworld Conference. The Mini, with more than 100,000 preorders, was a success before it was released on the market.

big release day came, the Mini sold out in stores across the nation within twenty-four hours.

Perhaps conscious of its critics, Apple then released its cheapest iPod yet. The Shuffle was launched on January 11, 2005. The new player was the size of a pack of gum and cost $99 for the version with a 512MB storage capacity and $129 for the 1GB model. To keep the player small, Apple did away with the LCD display and the hard drive, using a flash memory chip instead. Although the larger Shuffle could only hold about 250 songs, its tiny size appealed to those who wanted a lightweight MP3 player for exercising, travel, and other activities where even the Mini was deemed too large.

Because of its limited storage, the Shuffle was promoted for its ability to arbitrarily choose songs. Ad slogans for the Shuffle stated, "Enjoy uncertainty," "Life is random," "Choose to lose control."[30] While every iPod was capable of shuffling songs, the tiny Shuffle was seen by fans as the ultimate tool for random listening. Andy, a Shuffle owner, explains how the music player's arbitrary choice of song can influence his feelings as he walks through the city:

> I find that my iPod "colors" my surrounding quite significantly; as it's on shuffle I don't know what's coming up next, and it often surprises me how the same street can look lively and busy and colorful one moment and then—when a different song starts—it can change to a mysterious and unnerving place. I like the sensation, though.[31]

Even as the Shuffle helped Apple ring up record sales, the company continued to introduce innovative and unique MP3 players. In keeping with its tradition of releasing new products before the Christmas shopping season, Apple released the Nano, another mini-music player, in September 2005. The Nano was designed with a touch wheel to look like a larger iPod, but it did not have a Toshiba hard drive. Instead, the Nano worked with a high-capacity flash memory. The first generation was available in 2GB and 4GB capacity in either a black or white case.

The iPod Becomes Classic

With the introduction of the new minimodels, the original iPod was now seen as a large model. But it continued to improve every year. The fourth generation, launched in 2004, had stronger batteries that could last twelve hours between charges. The click wheel, made famous by the Mini, was included on the fourth-generation iPod and hard-drive storage capacity continued to grow. Consumers could buy 20-gigabyte models for $299 and double their storage capacity to 40 gigabytes for only $100 more.

With more hard-drive capacity, iPods could hold a greater number of files and run more-complicated operating systems. This allowed Apple to introduce the groundbreaking fourth-generation iPod in October 2004. This device took MP3 players into a new realm. With a color LCD display, users could browse through photo albums stored on their iPods.

BITS & BYTES

75%

Percentage of MP3 players sold worldwide in 2008 that were iPods

A special cable to connect the iPod to a television was available for about twenty dollars. With this feature, user-created slide shows could be played on a TV, complete with a soundtrack provided by the iPod song files. The color display also showed album covers for songs while they played.

In late 2005 the marketing and engineering genius behind the iPod was readily apparent. Apple announced that its profits had quadrupled due to iPod sales. In early 2006 the company stated that an astounding 32 million iPods had been sold in the previous year, one every second. Combined with sales figures from early years, it was clear that Apple controlled 75 percent of the MP3 player market.

Apple's reputation only continued to grow with the introduction of the fifth-generation device, the iPod video. With this iPod, users could watch videos in the MP4 format, a type of movie format based on Apple's QuickTime software. Using the adapter plug, the videos could also be shown on TVs. The new iPod was 30 percent thinner and had a brighter display and longer-lasting batteries than previous models.

Environmental Concerns

Environmentalists believe iPods contribute to air and water pollution. One of the main criticisms of players is the permanent batteries. While iPod's lithium batteries can be replaced, it is a difficult and costly procedure. That means that iPod owners often toss the player into the garbage can when the batteries die. And according to the environmental group Greenpeace, iPods are made with toxic chemicals, such as flame retardants, heavy metals, and polyvinyl chloride that pollute the environment when left in landfills. In addition, chemicals used in the earbuds, called phthalates, have been found to cause reproductive diseases and deformities in animals and humans. Responding to criticism, Apple launched an iPod recycling program in 2005, encouraging owners to bring their digital music players to Apple stores for free, environmentally friendly disposal. However, in 2009 only about 38 percent of old iPods were recycled. While many worn-out players remained in people's homes, millions of iPods ended up in landfills where their toxic chemicals polluted the environment. Similar problems have been reported with Zune and other MP3 players.

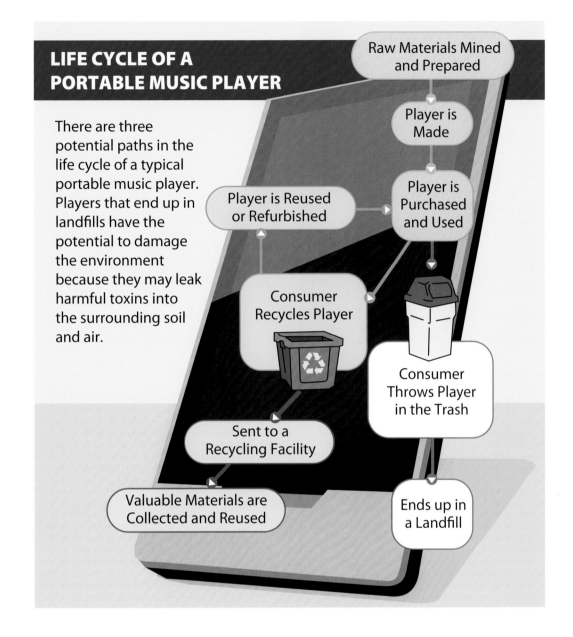

LIFE CYCLE OF A PORTABLE MUSIC PLAYER

There are three potential paths in the life cycle of a typical portable music player. Players that end up in landfills have the potential to damage the environment because they may leak harmful toxins into the surrounding soil and air.

Raw Materials Mined and Prepared

Player is Made

Player is Purchased and Used

Player is Reused or Refurbished

Consumer Recycles Player

Consumer Throws Player in the Trash

Sent to a Recycling Facility

Valuable Materials are Collected and Reused

Ends up in a Landfill

The sixth-generation, traditional iPod, was renamed the Classic when it was released in September 2007. Within two years, consumers could purchase a Classic with a 160GB storage capacity for $229.

When the old-style iPod became the Classic, Apple introduced the Touch, an MP3 player unlike any other previously seen. The most innovative aspect of the Touch is the source of

its name. The Touch has what is called a multitouch interface, which allows users to select music, videos, photos, and TV shows by touching the screen. Later models featured voice control so users could simply speak commands such as "Shuffle," "Pause," or "Next Song." They could also ask for the name of the song currently playing.

A Modest Competitor

Although Apple dominated the MP3 player market throughout the first decade of the twenty-first century, others tried to profit from the public enthusiasm for MP3 players. Sony, the company that helped launch the portable music era in the 1980s, began selling a line of digital Walkmans around the time the iPod was first released. However, these Walkmans did not play songs in the popular MP3 format.

Steve Jobs presents the new iPod Touch in 2008. The new product allowed users to select multimedia with the touch of their finger to the screen.

Users had to convert their MP3s to Sony's ATRAC format to use the players. In addition, instead of a simple name, like iPod, the player was called the ATRAC HDD Walkman and referred to by its serial number NW-HD1. With the clunky name and ATRAC format, Sony failed to compete with iPod.

Microsoft was also caught off guard by the success of the iPod. However, the company was well known for its Windows operating system, used by billions of people. Therefore, there was great public interest when company founder Bill Gates introduced the Zune MP3 player in November 2006. The 30-gigabyte Zune was similar to the iPod Classic with a few slight variations. The 3-inch (7.6 cm) screen was larger than the iPod's display, which made the Zune slightly taller and heavier. The Zune also had an FM radio, which iPod did not have at the time, and used a standard USB cord, rather than the dock connector. However, many critics complained that the Zune only worked with Microsoft operating systems, meaning it could not be used by Macintosh owners. In addition, the first-generation Zune only played music. It could not play videos or be used to import photos. It also lacked the calendars, contacts, and games that were standard on the iPod.

There was no Zune equivalent to an 80-gigabyte iPod, the Nano, or Shuffle. Perhaps this is what prompted Gates to call the iPod "phenomenal, unbelievable, fantastic" in front of an audience at Stanford University in California about a month after launching the Zune. Gates also downplayed expectations about the Zune, calling it a "modest"[32] competitor to the iPod. The public agreed. In 2008 only 2 percent of the MP3 players sold were Microsoft Zunes while 73 percent were iPods.

The iPod faced modest competition from products like the Sony Walkman, right, and Microsoft's Zune, left. Neither have affected the iPod's massive market share.

In 2009 Microsoft launched the touch-screen Zune HD that offered playback of high-definition movies and TV shows. The Zune HD also had games, supported audiobooks, and a Wi-Fi function called Zune-to-Zune. This allowed users to sync the device with computers and use it with a wireless network, wireless multiplayer gaming, and wireless shopping. The player could be controlled by the Zune Pad, a touch-sensitive button with improved navigation qualities but, again, the player could only be used on PCs. Critics continued to make negative comparisons with the Touch, but as *New York Times* technology critic David Pogue points out, "if this thing came out in a parallel universe where the iPod didn't exist, it would be hailed as a god."[33]

Despite the improvement, Zunes made up only 1.1 percent of all MP3 players sold in 2009. This was far behind even the SanDisk Sansa line of inexpensive MP3 players, which occupied over 8 percent of the market. Despite Microsoft's multimillion-dollar investment in the Zune, it could not compete with the iPod mystique. Levy writes, "[in] this age, at this moment, the iPod was . . . the perfect thing."[34]

CHAPTER 3

File-Sharing Frenzy

In September 2009 Apple announced it had sold a total of 220 million iPods. Meanwhile 8.5 billion songs had been downloaded through the iTunes Store. These figures prompted analysts to divide the number of songs sold by the number of iPods on the market. The resulting number revealed that the average iPod user had legitimately purchased only 36 songs from iTunes. Other song sales services were available, and many users uploaded their personal CD collections onto their players. However, the figures led music industry watchers to conclude that countless millions were filling their MP3 players with illegally downloaded songs. On the iPods Are Our Foes Web site, a poster known as the Stealin' Kind, who owns a 60GB iPod, writes, "I am not here to criticize or condone illegal music downloading, but just think, [my iPod holds] up to 15,000 songs. How many people would you expect to pay $15,000 to fill their iPods?"[35]

According to figures released by the music industry trade group International Federation of the Phonographic Industry (IFPI) in 2008, 40 billion songs were downloaded illegally, which is almost 30 songs for every Internet user worldwide. That year, even Steve Jobs had to admit that only 3 percent of music on the average iPod was purchased from the iTunes Store. Apple began selling the first iPods during the height of the Napster file-sharing fad. As billions of files were illegally downloaded, hundreds of millions of iPods were purchased by consumers. In his book, *The Big Switch: Rewiring the World from Edison to Google* author Nicholas Carr writes that digital music and digital music players were used together to perpetrate "the greatest . . . [overindulgence] of looting in history."[36]

Searching the World

Napster software initiated the wave of online looting. But by the time the company was shutdown by a court order in 2001, millions of people were well acquainted with the mechanics of downloading free music. In Napster's wake, new peer-to-peer (P2P) sites, such as Morpheus, Bear Share, Grokster, Kazaa, and LimeWire, began to attract millions of former Napster users. Having learned from Napster's mistakes, these Web sites conducted business differently. Napster had maintained a central server with lists of files users could access from other Napster users. Because of its centralized system, it was easy for music companies to pull the plug on Napster. But the new P2P programs allowed users to communicate with one another directly. This means that P2P file sharing is decentralized. It would be impossible for music companies to force millions of P2P users to stop using their personal computers to share music. A student named David at Southern Illinois University explains the difference between Napster and the P2P sites that followed:

> With Napster you could cast a shallow net looking for music, because you were restricted to how many other people were using Napster. There was a limited number of fish you could catch. With these other programs, you weren't just restricted to people using that program. You could look all over the world for all these different files from different programs. It was an exponential increase in what you could do and how much music you could get.[37]

BITS & BYTES

33%

Percentage of all Internet traffic in 2002 traced to people using BitTorrent software to share files

CENTRALIZED VS. DECENTRALIZED NETWORKS

Napster had allowed users to download music from a central or main server. Because the music files were managed from a single location, it was fairly simple to shut the business down. Unlike the central system, the peer-to-peer (P2P) system allows users to share music directly from multiple computers. There is no central server to arrest in this case, making it difficult for authorities to stop the millions of P2P users from sharing files.

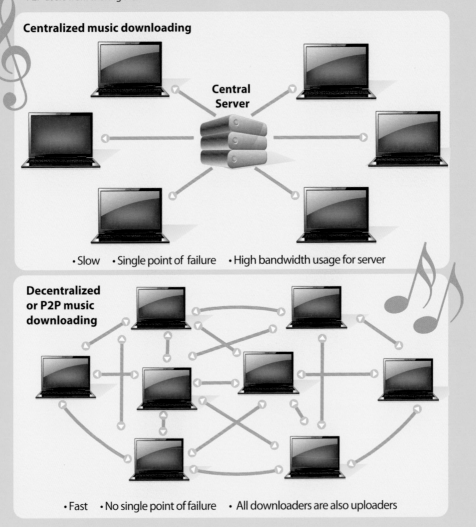

Centralized music downloading

Central Server

• Slow • Single point of failure • High bandwidth usage for server

Decentralized or P2P music downloading

• Fast • No single point of failure • All downloaders are also uploaders

So even as the record industry celebrated Napster's demise, interest in P2P file sharing was growing rapidly. In 2002 the most popular service, Kazaa, was averaging over 9 million users a month. By the following year, the number of people using all file-sharing services had exploded to 57 million in the United States alone. Together, Americans were downloading 2 billion music files monthly. And even Kazaa became obsolete when a new P2P file-sharing protocol called BitTorrent was introduced.

BitTorrent was invented by a twenty-six-year-old computer programmer named Bram Cohen in 2001. As the fastest, most-efficient, file-sharing system to date, BitTorrent works when computer users make files, or seeds, available for downloading. Those who want to access the seeds, called peers, can download the files which become seeds for others. Rather than downloading a song from a single source by using a program like LimeWire, BitTorrent downloads digital bits of songs from hundreds of seeders at once. The nature of BitTorrent allows for the rapid, or viral, spreading of files large and small. Entire albums can be downloaded in seconds while movies, TV shows, and software programs may take thirty minutes to several hours depending on how many people have seeded the file.

With its lightning-fast speeds, it is little wonder that BitTorrent spread rapidly. By 2003 more than one-third of all Internet traffic was traced to people using BitTorrent to share files. To many analysts it was clear that the music and movie industries had lost control of the products they produced. In a move to slow this trend, the RIAA once again went to court. The trade group sued StreamCast Networks, the company behind Grokster and Morpheus. However, in 2003 Judge Stephen Wilson ruled that StreamCast could not be held responsible for copyright infringement. Instead,

Music sharing sites followed a sharing protocol called a BitTorrent, which allows for rapid downloads. It highlighted to music and movie industry people that they had lost control of their own products.

Wilson writes, "individual users are accountable for illegally uploading and downloading copyrighted works off publicly accessible peer-to-peer networks."[38]

Gathering Evidence, Preparing Lawsuits

Although the RIAA failed to shut down Morpheus, the trade group was encouraged. Judge Wilson had made it clear that individuals were responsible for copyright infringement. In response to that finding, the RIAA took out a full-page ad in the *New York Times* on June 27, 2003, which read,

> Next time you or your kids "share" music on the Internet, you may also want to download a list of attorneys. . . . Starting today, the record industry will begin gathering evidence and preparing lawsuits against individual computer users who illegally "share" copyrighted music over so-called peer-to-peer networks. Some folks ask us, "How can you sue your consumers?" Well, the same question can be asked of retailers who prosecute shoplifters.[39]

Several months after the ad ran, the RIAA announced its first lawsuits, bringing charges against 261 people. The RIAA claimed that each individual had uploaded more than one thousand songs on P2P Web sites. Depending on the music located on their hard drives, they were sued for $750 to $150,000 per song, with number-one hits considered most valuable.

Some of the lawsuits reflected poorly on the RIAA and did little to garner sympathy for the record companies. One case targeted twelve-year-old Brianna LaHara, an honor student who lived in a New York City housing project. Brianna's mother, Sylvia Torres, had paid $29.95 for Brianna to use Kazaa. Torres thought the fee meant she was paying for the right to download music. The lawsuit made headlines across the country and Brianna was widely quoted as saying "I got really scared. My stomach is all turning. . . . I thought it was OK to download music because my mom paid a service fee for it. Out of all people, why did they pick me?"[40] Rather than fight a costly lawsuit, Torres settled with the RIAA for a $2,000 fine, which was paid by a sympathetic disc jockey.

A daughter and her parents face legal action for illegally downloading material online. They believed the material had been paid for through access to a downloading service.

As part of the settlement, Brianna was forced to publicly apologize. She said, "I am sorry for what I have done. I love music and don't want to hurt the artists I love."[41]

The publicity surrounding such lawsuits temporarily slowed file sharing. However, the media focus on cases like Brianna's hurt, rather than helped, the RIAA. Although it was stung by criticism, the RIAA continued to pursue file sharing. By 2007 the total number of people sued by the trade group reached thirty thousand. While most were university students, the RIAA also pursued expensive litigation against single mothers on welfare, disabled veterans, and children as young as seven years old. Dozens of people were driven into bankruptcy by the lawsuits.

Paying Thousands for Downloading

The Electronic Frontier Foundation (EFF) defends freedom of speech on the Internet. In recent years the group has been fighting what it calls the RIAA's "irrational war" on P2P file sharing, which it says has not stopped downloading but instead singled out a few people for a disproportionate punishment, forcing "ordinary Americans to pay thousands of dollars to music . . . industry lawyers." The foundation's Web site lists examples of people whose lives have been devastated by RIAA lawsuits:

> Take, for example, the case of the Tammy Lafky, a 41-year-old sugar mill worker and single mother in Minnesota. Because her teenage daughter downloaded some music—an activity both mother and daughter believed to be legal—Lafky faced over $500,000 in penalties.

The RIAA offered to settle for $4,000, but even that sum was well beyond Lafky's means—she earned just $21,000 per year and received no child support. . . .

> In yet another instance, Cassi Hunt, a student at M.I.T. [Massachusetts Institute of Technology in Cambridge, Massachusetts,] sued for illegally sharing music, attempted to negotiate the RIAA's proposed settlement price of $3,750. Hunt pointed out that she was already in debt to cover tuition. The RIAA's response? Its representative suggested that she drop out of school in order to pay off the settlement.

Electronic Frontier Foundation, "RIAA v. The People: Five Years Later," Electronic Frontier Foundation, September 2008, www.eff.org/wp/riaa-v-people-years-later#4.

Critics charged that the RIAA campaign unfairly singled out a few people, and their punishment was disproportionate for violating copyright laws. In 2006 a judge in Brooklyn, New York, agreed saying a record company's copyright is worth seventy cents per song, not the thousands of dollars per song charged in lawsuits. Despite the judge's finding, the RIAA lawsuits continued.

While some were forced to pay large sums to the RIAA, the group's ongoing campaign did little to stop illegal downloading. A 2007 survey by Piper found that about two-thirds of high school students who own MP3 players obtain music online through P2P networks.

iTunes: A Legal Alternative

Back in 2003, Steve Jobs expressed his thoughts on illegal downloading in a *Rolling Stone* magazine interview. He said,

> It's just wrong to steal. Or, let's put it another way: it is corrosive to one's character to steal. We want to provide a legal alternative. And we want to make it so compelling that all those people out there who really want to be honest, and really don't want to steal, but haven't had a choice if they wanted to get their music online, will now have a choice.[42]

There was little doubt that P2P file sharing would remain popular despite his words. But Jobs felt Apple could profit from the controversies swirling around copyright infringement and RIAA lawsuits. In the interview Jobs mentions the iTunes Store, calling it a legal alternative to file sharing. Opened on April 28, 2003, the store initially offered around two hundred thousand songs for downloading. During its first five days of operation, the store sold over 1 million songs for ninety-nine cents each. This was more songs than had been legally downloaded since the invention of the Internet. And the stunning popularity of the iTunes Store continued to grow after Apple launched a Windows version of iTunes in October, which made iPods compatible with PCs.

Within a year, Apple acquired permission to offer music produced by the four biggest record companies. These companies—Universal Music Group, Sony Music Entertainment, Warner Music Group, and EMI Group—controlled over 80 percent of the music market in 2004. In order to offer music produced by them, Apple had to design a security system to protect copyrights. This system, called digital rights management (DRM), had to prevent a downloaded song from being shared with those who did not pay for it. Apple's version of DRM was called FairPlay. It worked by encrypting each song purchased through the iTunes Store with a secret code. The code was stored on the user's iTunes Store account and on his or her computer and iPod.

The FairPlay code prevents a song from playing on unauthorized computers. It can, however, legally be played on five authorized computers and an unlimited number

The iTunes Store uses a digital rights management system to prevent people from downloading files they have not paid for.

of iPods. The song can be burned to a CD, although DRM coding lowers the sound quality. FairPlay encryption created great controversy because songs purchased from the iTunes Store could not be played on Zunes or other MP3 players.

Despite the restrictions created by FairPlay, the iTunes Store attracted a record number of new customers with its expanded catalog of over 2 million tunes and hundreds of thousands of songs were purchased every month. To encourage sales, Apple held a contest in 2004 to award prizes to the person who downloaded the 100 millionth song. On July 12, 2004, Apple announced, "Kevin Britten of Hays, Kansas downloaded Somersault (Dangermouse remix) by Zero7; the 100 millionth song purchased from the iTunes music store. He will receive a 17-inch PowerBook, a 40 [gigabyte] iPod, and a gift certificate for 10,000 iTunes songs to create the ultimate music library for his new iPod."[43]

By the time the iTunes Store celebrated its fifth anniversary, more than 4 billion songs had been downloaded from the site. By September 2009 that number had grown to 8.5 billion, 70 percent of all legal downloads worldwide. At that time the site offered 10 million songs.

Analysts link the popularity of the iTunes Store to its compatibility with the iPod and iTunes software. This compatibility allowed iPod users to simply click on the iTunes Store icon in their iTunes program, search for the songs desired, and instantly download the music. Since the store keeps customer and credit card information in the users account, there is no need for the user to fill out an order form with each purchase. The downloaded song goes straight into the iTunes library and instantly loads onto the user's iPod when it is connected to the computer. When the iPod Touch went on sale in September 2007, users did not even need a computer to use the iTunes Store. The Touch is sold with built in Wi-Fi capabilities allowing users to access the store with a wireless connection.

Dissolving the Album

Record companies generally earned around sixty-six cents from every ninety-nine-cent song sold by the iTunes Store. This was a much greater percentage of profit than they received from selling CDs, which had to be produced and shipped to record stores. While Apple only made a few cents per song, the iTunes Store helped spur iPod sales.

Despite an increase in single song sales, recording artists reported mixed feelings about the iTunes Store. Music makers had relied on sales of multisong albums since the late 1960s. As a result, musicians spent countless hours deciding which songs to include on an album and what their sequence should be. They did not appreciate people shuffling the songs or only buying one or two from an album. *New Yorker* magazine music critic David Denby commented, "If you reprogram the order of the cuts in a pop album, you dissolve the album, at least as the album was once conceived—as a story the artist wanted to tell."[44] Of course songs on CDs could be played in random order, but there was another reason recording artists did not like the surge in single song sales. Since the 1980s, consumers had been complaining that many CDs only contained a few good songs. The rest were seen as filler. The iTunes Store allowed music fans to purchase only the songs they wanted, spending two or three dollars per song, which denied recording artists the profits they previously made on an entire CD.

The iTunes Store also provided some artists with a new method to market their music. For example, in 2004 Liz Phair played a spontaneous three-song concert at the Chicago, Illinois, Apple store. The songs were soon offered on iTunes where they were purchased by about fifty thousand people.

"Treating Your Audience Like Thieves Is Absurd"

The alternative country band Wilco discovered that big sales can follow free downloads. In 2001 the group released their album *Yankee Hotel Foxtrot* for free on file-sharing networks. When it was subsequently released on CD four months later, it sold more copies than previous Wilco albums. In a 2004 *Wired* magazine interview, Wilco front man Jeff Tweedy explained his feelings about people sharing music on file-sharing networks:

A piece of art is not a loaf of bread. When someone steals a loaf of bread from the store, that's it. The loaf of bread is gone. When someone downloads a piece of music, it's just data until the listener puts that music back together with their own ears, their mind, their subjective experience. How they perceive your work changes your work.

Treating your audience like thieves is absurd. Anyone who chooses to listen to our music becomes a collaborator.

People who look at music as commerce don't understand that. They are talking about pieces of plastic they want to sell, packages of intellectual property.

I'm not interested in selling pieces of plastic.

Quoted in Xeni Jardin, "Music Is Not a Loaf of Bread," *Wired*, November 15, 2004, www.wired.com/culture/lifestyle/news/2004/11/65688?currentPage=2.

It would have been unprofitable for a large record company to produce and market a CD of the songs, but with the songs available for sale individually, fans were able to enjoy Phair's concert and she was able to earn some money in the process.

The Indie Marketplace

As Phair's experience shows, the iTunes Store permanently changed the way music is marketed. And the success of the iTunes Store helped pave the way for a new type of digital music marketing. Online sellers can bypass music controlled by large corporations and cater to smaller audiences. One of the more distinctive music sites, Amie Street, was created by three seniors at Brown University in Rhode Island in 2006. The store features about 850,000 titles from indie artists, those who are independent from major commercial record labels.

Amie Street is unique in that prices for downloads are determined by how popular a song is. Musicians upload a song onto the site, and if listeners like the song, they can recommend (REC) it to others. If the REC leads others to buy the song, the price increases from zero up to 98 cents. For example, as of 2007, if fifteen people bought a song, its price increased to 1¢. If twenty-five people bought it, its price increased to 15¢; 50 purchases resulted in 50¢, and 84 purchases resulted in 98¢. Artists receive 70 percent of the revenues from each song.

Competitors to Amie Street include SNOCAP, which helps musicians sell their songs through the social networking site MySpace. Another site, ReverbNation, offers "innovative marketing solutions that musicians need to compete, cooperate, and differentiate in an increasingly noisy online environment."[45] ReverbNation allows musicians to promote their music across the Internet though social networks, blogs, and the artist's home page.

Zune and Other Tunes

While independent music stores attract their share of fans, analysts continue to view Microsoft's Zune Marketplace, launched in 2006, as iTunes main competitor.

By 2009 Zune Marketplace offered over 5 million songs for owners of the Zune music player. The site functions much like iTunes but Microsoft offers a special deal called the Zune Pass. For $14.99 a month, consumers can download as many tunes as they want and permanently keep ten songs a month. However, if the subscriber stops paying the $14.99 fee, the songs disappear from the player's hard drive. *New York Times* technology critic David Pogue writes, "You could argue that those subscriptions are something of a ripoff; the day you stop paying that monthly fee, you lose your entire music collection."[46]

Another criticism is that Zune Marketplace only offers songs in a format called WMA, developed by Microsoft to compete with the MP4 format. Files in WMA, or Windows Media Audio, only play on Windows computers and Zunes. Therefore users cannot play their legally purchased songs on iPods or Macintosh computers. Analysts say the incompatibility issue is partially responsible for plummeting Zune sales. In 2008 Microsoft sold 54 percent fewer Zunes than in 2007.

Microsoft launched Zune Marketplace in 2006 to compete against Apple's iTunes. Zune Marketplace music files could only be played on the Zune, which affected its competitiveness.

The fact that the iTunes Store continued to dominate the digital music market did not stop others from offering downloadable music on their Web sites. Merchants such as Amazon.com and Wal-Mart offer downloadable music to consumers. Unlike the exclusive iTunes Store and Zune Marketplace, these sites sell songs in multiple formats, including WMA and MP3. And in late 2009 the search-engine giant Google also got into the MP3 business with its Discover Music Web site. Users can enter a song, artist, or album in the search engine, and Google takes them to sites such as Rhapsody, Lala, and iMeem where the songs can be heard and purchased.

Google Discovers Music

In October 2009 Google launched its Discover Music search engine which allows users to play millions of songs for free and directs consumers to sites where they can rent or purchase songs. Discover Music links to artists' home pages, Wikipedia entries, and related Web pages. The site was launched to compete with iTunes and one of the main beneficiaries of the site is Lala Media, a new company that allows users to listen to an entire album once for free before purchasing it.

An average of two of Google's top-ten search terms in any given week are music related. With the launch of Discover Music, record companies were hoping fans would be encouraged to pay for legal downloads. Thomas Hesse, president of digital music for Sony states, "We're trying to get consumers to interact with some of these more legitimate services. . . . Having Google step up and support this is a positive development."

Quoted in Alex Pham, "Google Sings a Different Tune with Its New Feature," *Los Angeles Times*, October 29, 2009.

The growth of online music stores meant the end of restrictions imposed by DRM. This was partially due to Steve Jobs, who had been campaigning to end the restrictions for several years. In an open letter dated February 6, 2007, Jobs notes that 20 billion songs were sold every year on CDs, which contain no DRM protections. He writes,

[If] the music companies are selling [the majority] of their music DRM-free [on CDs], what benefits do they get from selling the remaining small percentage of their music encumbered with a DRM system? There appears to be none. . . . If such requirements were removed, the music industry might experience an influx of new companies willing to invest in innovative new stores and players. This can only be seen as a positive by the music companies.[47]

Apple's iPod and iTunes Store are very popular with consumers and have made Apple a leader in the industry.

Jobs does not mention that many consumers were frustrated by the digital locks on the songs they purchased. As people upgraded their computers, the songs could not be transferred to the new hardware. Rather than pay for songs that were only playable on five devices, DRM restrictions drove consumers to continue downloading unrestricted songs. In 2009 this reality pushed the four biggest record companies to allow the iTunes Store to offer DRM-free songs for $1.29 each. Previously purchased songs could be upgraded for $0.30 each.

Out of Sight, Out of Mind

Despite the competition, Apple achieved record profits in 2009, proving the iPod and the iTunes Store remained exceedingly popular. And the store, along with other digital music retailers, became a driving force in the music industry. In 2008 digital downloads increased 27 percent over the previous year as 1 billion songs were downloaded. Although the majority of album sales were traditional CDs, analysts can see a day when they disappear from store shelves. As media analyst Richard Greenfield told the *New York Times*, "CDs no longer drive somebody into a store . . . as CDs really go out of sight, out of mind for the consumer."[48]

CHAPTER 4

Podcasts, Vodcasts, and Audiobooks

At the end of the twentieth century, large entertainment companies controlled the media sphere. They largely determined the music people would hear and the videos and movies the public would view. Executives and producers at RCA, Sony, Fox, Warner, MGM, and a few other corporations had held that power for decades. From the dawn of radio in the 1920s, to the introduction of television in the 1950s, and the growth of the Internet through the 1990s, if something was broadcast to the public, the content was usually provided by a major corporation. Because broadcast media had to reach the widest audience to be profitable, controversy was generally avoided along with media that might appeal to only a few thousand people. Then along came the digital media revolution.

With the introduction of MP3 players and inexpensive digital recording and editing software, professional and amateur musicians who wanted to distribute songs to a few people, or a few thousand, could easily do so. Experts in particular subjects from wine tasting to nuclear physics could record a program and share it with others. While these new programs could be played on any MP3 player, this new do-it-yourself media picked up the name podcasts because of the iPod's popularity.

Audio 2 Go

In 2001 when Steve Jobs, chief executive officer of Apple Inc., announced the "major, major breakthrough" of the iPod, the idea of using the Internet to broadcast a program in serial episodes, like radio or television shows, was not new. Webcasting, as it is called, was pioneered by tech writer Carl Malamud on April 1, 1993, when the Internet was in its infancy. Malamud often attended meetings where the world's leading engineers and computer programmers discussed ways to improve the Internet. He taped interviews with some of these high-tech pioneers and broadcast them on a show called *Geek of the Week*. Malamud's show had

A computer screen displays a podcast during the CNN/ YouTube Republican presidential debate in 2007. Podcasts first began in 2001 and can be listened to on MP3 players.

twenty to thirty thousand fans, but they had to be patient if they wanted to hear the broadcast; Internet connections were so slow in the early nineties that it might take listeners two hours to download a thirty-minute program.

Although such programs are now referred to as podcasts (after the iPod), Apple was not the first company to enable users to listen to programs on digital music players. The manufacturer of an earlier MP3 player, i2Go, was the first to launch an audio news and entertainment service for a portable digital device. In order to boost sales of their MP3 player eGo, the company introduced the service MyAudio2Go, in September 2000. The Web site provided radio-style shows with news, sports, entertainment, weather, and music. Users could download the shows and listen to them on the eGo players. However, i2Go pulled the plug on MyAudio2Go when the company went bankrupt in 2001.

RSS and iPod Magic

In 2000 broadband and wireless networks were just beginning to gain popularity. The majority of Internet users had dial-up connections which meant that loading a radio program for an MP3 player was a slow process. To deal with this problem, the eGo was programmed to download content overnight while the player was recharging. Adam Curry, a former MTV veejay, recognized that slow downloads were a problem, and he searched for solutions. Curry was enthusiastic about the broadcasting abilities of the World Wide Web, and he envisioned a system where huge files could easily download onto computer hard drives. Curry says,

> If the computer is always on and connected [to the Internet], why don't we drip stuff in as fast as we can get it? It will be relatively slow and not fast enough for [a] real-time streaming experience, but if you don't know you're waiting, it doesn't hurt. When it's there, bing! You have something new, and then you can open up a

BITS & BYTES

1 million

Number of podcasts downloaded in two days after the iTunes Store began offering the programs in 2005

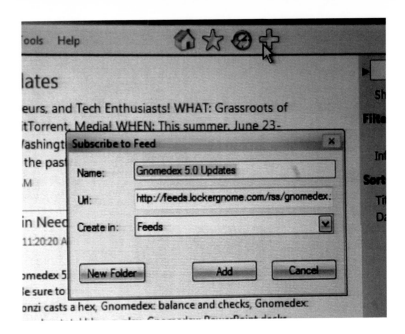

Users can subscribe to RSS feeds to receive information on their computers.

five-hundred-megabyte file, and the radio experience is going to be there.[49]

Curry, who was not a computer programmer, explained his idea to Dave Winer, a software designer he met at a party. Winer, a computer prodigy, was known for keeping a Web page journal called "Scripting News," about computer technology. Developed in 1997, "Scripting News" was read by major players in the computer industry, including Microsoft's chief executive officer, Bill Gates. Winer's Web journal, which was updated regularly and featured personal observations and information, is considered one of the first Web logs, or blogs.

Curry described his idea to Winer as a combination of blogging and broadcast radio. Winer had already developed a technology that he thought would work with radio blogging. Readers of "Scripting News" could subscribe to the blog just as they would a magazine. Each issue of the blog was delivered to subscribers in the middle of the night through digital files called feeds. The technology came to be known as Really Simple Syndication (RSS).

Winer modified RSS so that it could deliver digital audio files to subscribers. The first test of the system came on January 11, 2001, when Winer enclosed a song by the band the Grateful Dead in his "Scripting News" blog. Although few people understood RSS technology, blogging was becoming a major worldwide fad. Millions of average citizens became part of the phenomenon, and they were soon joined by politicians, newscasters, and celebrities.

In 2003 while countless bloggers were putting their thoughts into words with their keyboards, Curry bought his first iPod. He quickly realized that the sleek digital player would work perfectly with radio blogging. People could create audio files and users could subscribe to the feeds. RSS would automatically download them into iTunes which would then load the files onto an iPod when it was plugged into the computer. Curry explains, "We had this transport mechanism [RSS]—and here's the iPod. That was really the big wow factor, when the process was end to end. Someone publishes, it shows up on my iPod. It's magic."[50]

iPod Blogs

In his book *The Perfect Thing*, Steven Levy discusses the popularity of iPod blogs in 2003. He writes,

> Among Apple fans and tech watchers, blogs were often the launching pad for strange iPod-related multimedia expression: miniessays, love letters, and borderline psychotic object worship. People would design exotic "fantasy" iPods. In the days before a Steve Jobs presentation, the blogosphere would be abuzz with swooning speculations about what he might be unveiling. Though cynics sometimes debunked the phenomenon by charging that Apple actually seeded this rumor mill itself to crank up the buzz level to full blast, there is every indication that Steve Jobs wasn't happy about these speculations, especially when the predictions— apparently arrived at with the connivance of inside leakers—came close to the mark.

Steven Levy, *The Perfect Thing*, New York: Simon & Schuster, 2006, p. 238.

The Podcast Explosion

Curry was not the only person wowed by the iPod. At the time he thought of merging RSS with iTunes, there were millions of people already writing blogs about iPods. In fact, more bloggers were posting to the iPod category, or tag, than any other. People typed millions of words about the iPod, discussing technical facts, problems, loves, hates, newest models, and so on.

While the iPod rapidly grew in stature in the blogosphere, Winer was working to perfect RSS technology. He partnered with Christopher Lydon, a reporter and National Public Radio talk-show host, who had built a portable recording studio. Lydon used his studio to conduct interviews with politicians, tech intellectuals, and bloggers. After he completed twenty-five interviews, he released them on a subscription basis using Winer's RSS.

In February 2004 British reporter Ben Hammersley wrote about Lydon's interviews in the *Guardian*, a newspaper in the United Kingdom. Hammersley used the term *podcasting* to describe the shows and the method they were distributed through RSS feeds over the Internet. It is believed that blogger Danny Gregoire read Hammersley's column and registered the term *podcasting* as a domain name, a sequence of letters or words that describes a specific Internet address. Several months later, Curry was trying to think up the perfect term for audio blogging. He learned about Gregoire's domain name and said, "Yeah! That's it, *podcast*. . . . It's a sexy word, it was the right thing, and it just took off."[51]

The term *podcast* went viral, even as critics protested that podcasts were only MP3 or MP4 files that could be played on most computers and digital players. Curry argued that podcasts were based on iPods, since they were the most popular digital media players. Whatever the case, the numbers tell the story of the explosive growth of podcasting. In early September 2004 Google recorded 526 hits for the search term *podcast*. Within a month, that number had grown to 2,750 and began doubling every few days.

By the end of October, podcasts were featured in a *New York Times* story. The article mentions Curry's Web site which made free podcasting software available to the public. The *Times* also listed some of the most popular podcasts of the day, including a thirty-minute comedy called the *Dawn and Drew Show*, produced by a Wisconsin couple. Another popular podcast, the *Daily Source Code*, was produced by Curry and featured music, personal stories, and the latest information about podcasting.

Winer had his own podcast, *Morning Coffee News*, in which he discussed his latest ideas for software and technology. Winer recorded the show while driving his car, and his geeky commentary about source codes and Internet development was often interrupted with information about traffic jams, rude drivers, and truck stops.

While the eccentric innovators of podcasting were speaking to their fans, the concept quickly caught on with the public. Annalee Newitz, a reporter for *Wired* magazine, called

A university student records a podcast. The popularity of podcasts has grown rapidly, with millions being downloaded.

podcasting "the offspring of the blog and the Apple MP3 player,"[52] and Apple was quick to take advantage of the phenomenon. On June 28, 2005, when a new version of iTunes was released, podcast options were added to the iTunes Store. Instead of using RSS feeds, users could subscribe to, download, and organize podcasts through a simple iTunes function.

With Apple promoting podcasts, the fad exploded. Within two days of its launch, the updated iTunes Store showed that 1 million podcasts had been downloaded. Three months later, on September 28, 2005, Google reported more than 100 million searches for the word *podcast*. By March 2006 that number had more than doubled to 215 million. And this was only eighteen months after 526 searches were reported for podcasts. However, Zune users could not participate in the podcast phenomenon since the original players only worked with WMA files, which most podcasters did not provide to subscribers. And the software included with the original Zune did not allow users to find, subscribe to, or manage podcasts. This situation changed in 2007 when Zune software was updated to allow users to participate in podcasting.

Podcast Broadcasting

The podcast trend quickly proved to be as big as the blog phenomenon. Within a year, it seemed as if more people were creating podcasts than listening to them. In 2006 Yahoo! listed more than twenty-three thousand podcasts in its news category alone. Beyond current events, the number of podcast tags increased daily, and some of the producers were surprising. For example, Vatican Radio began providing religious podcasts, which were loaded onto a Nano and presented to Pope Benedict. In the months that followed, the pope himself could be heard on podcasts. Benedict was among thousands of Christian, Jewish, Hindu, Muslim, Buddhist, and even pagan spiritual leaders who were presenting their sermons on downloadable programs now referred to as "godcasts." Programs included the *Wired Jesus Broadcast* (for tech-savvy Christians), the *Pagan Power Hour* (information about casting magic spells), and *Zencast* (inspirational Buddhist talks).

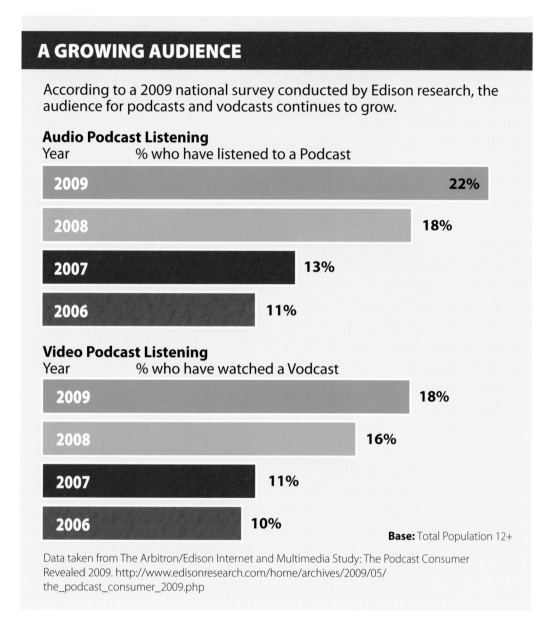

A GROWING AUDIENCE

According to a 2009 national survey conducted by Edison research, the audience for podcasts and vodcasts continues to grow.

Audio Podcast Listening

Year — % who have listened to a Podcast

Year	%
2009	22%
2008	18%
2007	13%
2006	11%

Video Podcast Listening

Year — % who have watched a Vodcast

Year	%
2009	18%
2008	16%
2007	11%
2006	10%

Base: Total Population 12+

Data taken from The Arbitron/Edison Internet and Multimedia Study: The Podcast Consumer Revealed 2009. http://www.edisonresearch.com/home/archives/2009/05/the_podcast_consumer_2009.php

In 2006 more than three thousand godcasts were listed on the iTunes Store under the burgeoning tag "Religion & Spirituality." In addition, the store listed fifteen other podcast categories: arts; business; comedy; education; games and hobbies; government and organizations; health; kids and family;

A vicar records a sermon on podcast in church. The iTunes Store offered more than 3,000 "godcasts" to users in 2006.

music; news and politics; science and medicine; society and culture; sports and recreation; technology; TV and film.

Anyone who wanted to become a podcast broadcaster could easily do so using Apple's GarageBand software. GarageBand was first released in 2004 as a program used to record music. GarageBand 3, launched in 2006, included a podcast studio function. This allowed creators to interview people using Apple's iChat software and integrate the track into the podcast. Podcasts could be made more exciting through the use of two hundred effects and jingles included with GarageBand. And after the program was completed, the podcast could be published, or uploaded, to iTunes with the click of a mouse.

While GarageBand led the way, many other free or inexpensive podcasting software programs were created and made available on the Internet. However, amateur podcasters found increasing competition from professional radio, TV, and cable media producers. Celebrities, rock musicians, and well-known entertainers also began creating their own podcasts, and these were the most popular shows. In 2009 when 21 million people, or 10 percent of all Internet users, were downloading one podcast per month, the shows that were consistently "top podcasts" on the iTunes Store were produced by recognizable entities, such as National Public Radio, HBO, and MSNBC.

A Record-Setting Podcast

Most people give their podcasts away for free, but Ricky Gervais does not do things like most people. Gervais is an English comedian known for creating the popular TV series *The Office* and the 2009 film *The Invention of Lying*. When he began producing podcasts of *The Ricky Gervais Show* in February 2006, the comedian decided to sell the thirty-minute episodes for about two dollars each. The show proved to be instantly popular, and people were willing to pay for it. During its first season, the weekly episodes were consistently number one on the iTunes download charts. While most other popular podcasts receive around 50,000 downloads, *The Ricky Gervais Show* had an average of 261,670 downloads per episode. As a result, the show entered the *Guinness Book of World Records* as the most popular podcast in the world with a total of 8 million downloads in 2006.

Vodcasting

Even before podcasts were available on the iTunes Store, Steve Jobs could see that video podcasts, or vodcasts, could become the next big thing. When he introduced the fifth-generation iPod video at the Macworld Conference & Expo in January 2005, Jobs showed a brief clip of a vodcast called *Tiki Bar TV*. The five-minute Canadian show featured bar patrons whose problems were instantly solved by the cocktails prescribed by a character named Dr. Tiki. The show was produced in the tiny Vancouver, Canada, apartment of filmmaker Jeff Macpherson.

After Jobs debuted the clip, *Tiki Bar TV* became a cult sensation jumping from ten thousand downloads to hundreds of thousands overnight. However, vodcasting was much more difficult than podcasting. Each short episode of *Tiki Bar TV* required about six hours of production time, and the show was provided for free. As Macpherson notes, vodcasting "doesn't make filmmaking any easier. There's no short cut to make things look good."[53]

Lack of production values did not slow the vodcast trend, however. According to Edison Research, the rise in vodcasting was as dramatic as podcasting. By 2008, 16 percent of all Americans over the age of eleven subscribed to vodcasts, 50 percent more than in the previous year. And the widespread availability of inexpensive video cameras and editing software helped propel the trend in vodcasting.

Rock bands posted music videos, self-described geeks expounded on technology, amateurs posted pet tricks, and animators created countless cartoons. Consumers could subscribe to vodcasts featuring sports, politics, comedy, travel, documentaries, film, and fashion. And, as with podcasts, professionals in the news and entertainment business made numerous vodcasts, too.

iTunes U

Some of the growth in vodcasting and podcasting can be traced to the field of education. As far back as 2004, every incoming freshman to Duke University in Durham, North Carolina, was given a free iPod. As the semesters progressed, the students were provided with podcasts and vodcasts of classroom lectures. Duke provost Peter Lange explains, "Imagine that instead of taking copious notes, you could go back to any lecture later on in the semester and find exactly what the professor was talking about. That's a clear educational use."[54]

The classroom podcast trend caught on with leading colleges and universities, including Stanford University and the University of California, Berkeley in California and the Massachusetts Institute of Technology in Massachusetts. While the initial podcasts were provided through campus Web sites, thousands of lectures were made available on the iTunes Store in 2007 when Apple launched iTunes U. The site features free educational content, such as course lectures, language lessons, lab demonstrations, sports highlights, and campus tours.

Access to the podcasts and vodcasts might be limited to students enrolled in a specific class, all matriculating students, or faculty members. Programs are also distributed to the general public with no limitations.

Few were surprised when iTunes U proved to be a dramatic overnight success. By October 2009 the site contained more than two hundred thousand educational files. In addition to providing daily lectures, professors use the site to publicize research projects. This allows them to share their knowledge with other researchers, financial donors, and the general public.

Professors who have posted lectures on iTunes U have been surprised to see their lessons receiving tens or even hundreds of thousands of downloads. And students have benefited as well. Research shows that students miss key points during class, and they perform better when they can review tapes or videos of the lesson. A February 2009 study, conducted by Dani McKinney, a psychologist at the State University of New York, demonstrates that students who watched a lecture on iTunes U scored an average of 71 percent on a post-lecture quiz. Students who sat through the thirty-minute classroom lecture but did not view the video scored an average of only 62 percent.

Amazon's CEO Jeff Bezos holds up a Kindle, a digital reading device on which users can read books and other materials.

Audiobooks

Some of the offerings available on iTunes U are provided in the form of audiobooks. These spoken word files of authors or celebrities reading published books have long been available on CDs and cassette tapes. In 1997 a company called Audible was the first to sell books for digital players, which the company also manufactured. In 2003 in order to quickly enter the audiobooks market, Apple bought Audible's catalog of books and set up an audiobooks segment on the iTunes Store.

By 2008 iTunes had over twenty thousand audiobooks for sale. They ranged from $40 offerings by best-selling author Stephen King to $5.95 classics, such as *Winnie the Pooh* and *Dracula*. A "Meet the Author" section connected listeners to the podcasts made by top authors who discuss the season's hottest books and related topics.

While the iTunes Store helped popularize audiobooks, there are many other places to find books for digital media players. In 2009 the company that started the trend, Audible, had sixty thousand audiobooks, and the site Simply Audio Books offers memberships for a low fee that includes unlimited audiobook rentals.

Multimedia Mayhem

The popular star Tyrese is known as an MTV veejay, a fashion model, a movie star, and a rapper and R&B singer. In September 2009 Tyrese found another outlet for his creative energies. He developed his own comic book series called Mayhem. But instead of printing the comic book in the traditional manner, he worked with Apple to create a digital experience available on the iTunes Store. When the first-ever interactive comic appeared, it was downloadable with ear-blasting sound effects, page turns, and voiceover narration. Those who purchased the comic for their digital media players also received a forty-five-minute making-of-Mayhem video, alternate covers, concept art, and desktop wallpapers. Commenting on his move into the new world of digital comics, Tyrese told CNN, "There's this digital revolution that's out there but the comic book world has not embraced this digital revolution on a level that it should be embraced on. And so I reached out . . . and this is my baby."

Quoted in Jack Hannah, "Singer-Actor Tyrese Invents Comic Book Superhero," CNN, September 30, 2009, www.cnn.com/2009/SHOWBIZ/Music/09/29/tyrese .gibson.comics/index.html.

Those who would rather read books than listen to them have found that their iPods and Zunes can be useful tools with e-books. Also called electronic books, these digitized files in book form can be uploaded onto media players. Amazon.com attracted a great deal of attention to e-books when it launched the Kindle in November 2007. The $399 digital reading device with a 6-inch (15.2cm) screen sold out in five and a half hours.

New Worlds of Media

When the tech teams at Apple were busily designing the iPod in 2000, even a visionary like Steve Jobs could not imagine the massive public interest the player would generate for podcasts, vodcasts, and audiobooks. While Apple led with the technology, millions of do-it-yourself podcast producers used their creative talents to change what was possible. By reshaping the boundaries of the iPod, they also transformed culture. Before the podcast revolution, people listened to a few dozen radio stations where the content was picked by an elite group of producers. After podcasts flooded the Internet, people could hear and view a nearly infinite variety of free and commercial-free programs to suit their mood. And while the iTunes Store remained the number-one site for downloads, interest in podcasting and audiobooks enlarged the marketplace with hundreds of businesses taking advantage of the boom.

There is little doubt that the iPod and other players transformed the concept of media in the twenty-first century. And in doing so the small electronic devices opened a portal into new worlds of education, entertainment, current events, and even spirituality.

CHAPTER 5

The Next Generation

When MP3 players were first introduced in the late 1990s, they were seen as compact, music-listening devices comparable to portable CD players. There were disadvantages to early MP3 players, because they held a limited number of songs and the song files could only be preloaded using a computer. But with their small size and solid-state circuitry, which prevented skipping, MP3 players began to appeal to a small number of consumers.

Few people outside the computer industry thought MP3 players would ever do more than simply play songs. But in the 2000s, the digital audio player was transformed. With the iPod leading the way, the player became a multimedia device capable of shooting pictures and videos and playing movies and TV shows as well as songs. But perhaps the most dramatic transition took place when the multimedia functions of the digital audio player were combined with the cell phone. This merging of technologies created smartphones, which are expected to make up one-quarter of all cell-phone sales by 2013.

Smartphones Before the iPod

The first smartphone, called the Simon Personal Communicator, was launched in 1994, four years before the first

MP3 player was introduced. The Simon combined the features of a mobile phone, a pager, and a fax machine and contained a calendar, address book, world clock, calculator, e-mail functions, and games. However, the phone cost thirteen hundred dollars in today's dollars and did not catch on with the public.

It was not until 2002 that smartphones began to gain popularity. The BlackBerry phone, developed by the Canadian company Research in Motion (RIM), had a keyboard and color display and supported e-mail, text messaging, Internet faxing, Web browsing, and other wireless information services. Because it was exceedingly popular in the high-powered corporate environment, the Black-Berry quickly became a cultural icon for status-conscious consumers. So many people began habitually checking their e-mail with their BlackBerrys that the smartphone earned the name CrackBerry, a reference to the addictive properties of crack cocaine. By 2006 the term was so widespread that *Webster's New World College Dictionary* named *crackberry* the new word of the year.

Also in 2006 RIM introduced the BlackBerry Pearl with a digital camera and a media player for both audio and visual files. The Pearl is what is called a convergent device, because it brings together a group of technologies that were formerly sold separately. A convergent device combines telecommunications, the Internet, and broadcast media in the form of downloadable music, video, and television functions. While people generally use different companies to provide them with Internet services, TV, radio, CDs, and telephones, convergent devices bring all these things together in the palm of the user's hand.

The BlackBerry smartphone is promoted on a city street corner. The popular BlackBerry allows access to phone, email, text messaging, Internet browsing, and other services.

Unexpected Uses for the iPod

Although the iPod was designed to play music and video files, people have changed the way the device is being used. The Open Culture Web site lists a few of the unexpected uses for the iPod. They are:

Train Doctors to Save Lives: iPods can double interns' ability to identify heart sounds that are indicative of serious heart problems. . . . By using the iPod to repeatedly listen to recordings of normal and abnormal heart beat patterns, interns can effectively hear when something is going awry. . . .

Throw a Meaner Curveball: Jason Jennings, a pitcher for the Houston Astros, started using a video iPod last year to review his pitching frame by frame and to improve his overall technique. He also reviews video of all opposing batters before each game.

Test Cheating: Yes, unfortunately technology can be used for bad as well as good. It was widely reported . . . that students are apparently using the iPod to cheat on exams. During tests, they'll apparently sneak earbuds into their ears and tap into valuable formulas, class notes, voices recordings, etc. Others will even write out crib notes and enmesh them within song lyrics.

Open Culture, "10 Unexpected Uses of the iPod," Open Culture, April 30, 2007, www.openculture .com/2007/04/10_unexpected_u.html.

Consumers value convergent devices because of their great convenience. And the popularity of the devices has also been extremely profitable to electronics manufactures, media producers, and telecommunications companies.

The iPhone

There was great anticipation in January 2007 when Steve Jobs, chief executive officer of Apple Inc., announced Apple's newest product, the iPhone, at the Macworld Conference & Expo. He said,

This is a day I've been looking forward to for two and a half years. Every once in a while a revolutionary product comes along that changes everything. . . . Today, we're introducing THREE revolutionary new products. The first one is a widescreen iPod with touch controls. The second is a revolutionary new mobile phone. And the third is a breakthrough internet communications device. . . . An iPod, a phone, an internet mobile communicator. . . . These are NOT three separate devices! And we are calling it iPhone! Today Apple is going to reinvent the phone.[55]

Apple designed the iPhone to run on OS X, the same operating system found on every Apple computer. This meant that for the first time a mobile phone could perform the exact functions of a desktop or laptop computer.

The iPhone was different from other smartphones because it did not have a little plastic keyboard. Instead, it was equipped with a multitouch screen that users could operate with their fingers. They could simply touch a button on the screen to bring up a touch-activated keyboard when needed. Another feature allowed the iPhone to sync with iTunes. This let users put their songs, videos, podcasts, photos, TV shows, movies, and audiobooks onto their phone. In addition, the phone worked as a personal digital assistant (PDA), syncing with a user's calendar, address book, e-mail addresses, browser bookmarks, and so on. The iPhone also had Wi-Fi capabilities, a built-in camera, a speaker, an input for a microphone, and a jack for stereo earphones.

Before the iPhone went on sale on June 29, 2007, buyers lined up for four days at the flagship New York City Apple store. People also camped out in San Francisco, California;

Attendants of the Macworld Conference and Expo 2007 examine the new iPhone, produced to compete with the BlackBerry and other smartphones.

The iPhone's software applications, called apps, range from educational to games. One of its most popular apps is the game Crash Bandicoot Nitro Kart 3D.

Portland, Oregon; and elsewhere. Some buyers were motivated by bloggers who referred to the iPhone as the Jesus phone because of its revolutionary design. The publicity was also phenomenal. Over eleven thousand articles were written about the phone between January and June and anyone who typed "iPhone" into Google came up with about 69 million hits.

The iPhone was an instant success, but there was criticism. One of the main problems pointed out by reviewers was that the iPhone batteries were not replaceable. Owners whose batteries died had to send their iPhones back to Apple for battery replacement at a cost of about $85. In a 2009 article in the *New York Times*, David Pogue writes, "The camera's terrible! . . . It can't record video! There's no voice dialing! No copy and paste! The iPhone can't even send picture messages—even $20 starter phones can do that!"[56] Apple fixed all those problems when it launched the iPhone 3G, which sold for $199 in 2009. Although it cost much less, the 3G was a major improvement over the first-generation iPhone because it operated on the 3G, or third generation, phone network.

3G was an updated telephone network that offered dramatically faster data transfer rates. This meant that iPhone 3G users not only had faster Web surfing and music downloads, but they could use their phones to stream media. Streaming allows users to watch full-length movies, provided by sites such as Netflix, as they are downloading onto the device. With the OS X operating system and 3G network speeds, the iPhone 3G essentially had the same capabilities as a desktop computer. Once again consumers responded with enthusiasm. On the first day of the July 11, 2009, launch, the iPhone 3G sold out in New York City, Los Angeles, Phoenix, Denver, Chicago, Boston, and many other cities.

Apple Apps

One of the reasons for the iPhone's popularity was the unprecedented versatility of its apps, or software applications, that included games, utilities, entertainment, and education functions. iPhone apps are sold through the iTunes App Store, launched in July 2008. By November 2009 owners of the iTouch and iPhone had downloaded more than 2 billion apps for free or for a small fee. At that time there were more than eighty-five thousand apps available, developed by thousands of software designers.

Some of the most popular apps include Crash Bandicoot Nitro Kart 3D, a $2.99 game that lets players twist and turn through race courses while battling opponents. Apps such as Flixster allow users to watch movie trailers, get show times, and share movie ratings with friends. Other entertainment apps let users read horoscopes or play solitaire. Some apps have more practical uses. The Flashlight, when activated, fills the screen of the Touch or iPhone with bright white light for use in emergencies. Other utilities include a tip calculator for restaurants and even a tuner so musicians can get their guitars in tune.

Inside Apple Apps

Apple encouraged the proliferation of iPhone and iTouch apps by making a software development kit (SDK) available in February 2008. The SDK allows developers to design, test, and distribute apps through the iTunes App Store. Developers can release the app for free or charge a fee. Apple takes a 30 percent share of profits made from sales while the developer is paid 70 percent. The SDK is available on Apple's iPhone Development Center Web site, which also provides videos on tools, technologies, and software coding.

MONTHLY DOWNLOADS BY DEVICE

A 2010 survey published by advertising firm AdMob Mobile found that iPod Touch® users download more applications or "apps" than iPhone® and Google Android® users. According to the survey, 65 percent of iPod Touch users are under the age of 17 and on average Touch users spend more time using the apps than smartphone users.

Product	Number of Downloads (per month)	Percentage of users under 17	Percentage of users 18 and older
iPod Touch®	12.1	65%	35%
iPhone®	8.8	13%	87%
Google Android®	8.7	7%	93%

Data taken from: http://metrics.admob.com/wp-content/uploads/2010/02/AdMob-Mobile-Metrics-Jan-10.pdf

Using apps, consumers find recipes, shop at their favorite stores, look up words or song lyrics, find the cheapest gas, or check their bank balances. Software pertaining to sports, music, videos, photography, weather, medicine, tourism, and fitness can be accessed with the touch of a finger. With these applications added to their digital media devices, users can perform a wide array of tasks without ever touching a notebook or desktop computer.

Google Android

By the end of 2009, Apple had sold 21.4 million iPhones. However, like the iPod, the iPhone's success made it a target for competitors. RIM brought out the BlackBerry

Storm, the first model of its popular phone with a touch screen replacing the traditional keypad. Reviews of the Storm were mixed. Critics pointed out that the phone was about 15 percent heavier and thicker than the iPhone. But the Storm compared favorably to the iPhone because it had replaceable batteries, cut and paste functions, and superior voice dialing features. However, the browser was slow and prone to error while the operating system would abruptly freeze and reboot. These problems prompted Pogue to call the Storm a "buggy, sluggish, counterintuitive mess."[57]

When RIM launched the Storm 2 in October 2009, many of these problems were fixed. And the Storm 2, and other new smartphones such as the HTC Hero, ran on Android software developed by Google. Before the introduction of Android, most non-Apple smartphones ran on Microsoft's Windows Mobile operating system which cost phone manufacturers fifteen to twenty dollars per phone. However, Google provides Android for free, and it has several features that are attractive to cell-phone

Motorola introduced the Droid smartphone in 2009 to compete directly against the iPhone.

makers. Android is intended for modern screens that people tap with their fingers, while Windows Mobile was built for use with a stylus. Android is open source software, so anyone can use or change it. This has encouraged thousands of software designers to create over fifteen thousand applications, or apps, available at the Google's Android Market.

In September 2009 Motorola launched the Droid, a thin phone that uses the Android operating system. It can be used like an iPod, playing audio and video files and podcasts, and it contains a camera with DVD-quality video recording. The Droid was sold exclusively in the United States by Verizon, which ran a series of advertisements heavily critical of the iPhone. Verizon ads stated, "iDon't have a real keyboard, iDon't run simultaneous apps. . . . Everything iDon't—Droid Does."[58] While Jobs introduced the iPhone as a superior device because it did not have a keyboard, the Droid was promoted for having keys which made it easier to use.

Because of their many multimedia and Internet functions, phones such as the Droid were increasingly in demand by 2009. Analysts predict the smartphone market will grow at about 30 percent a year to 180 million units by 2011. That is expected to exceed the number of notebook computers sold annually, and according to tech reviewer Brian X. Chen in *Wired* magazine, "that would suggest smartphones are shaping up to become the next major computing platform—and the companies who control the dominant platforms stand to gain billions in revenue."[59]

High Definition

Smartphones and newer digital media players allow people to access almost every page and file on the World Wide Web. However, few have the patience to watch a feature-length film on the 3.5-inch (8.9cm) screen common on most smartphones. In order to enhance the viewing experience, some consumers are turning to portable media centers (PMC). While few predict that PMCs will replace iPods for listening to music, media centers are brighter, clearer, and more versatile than smartphones and digital media players.

One example of the new wave in PMCs is the Archos 5 Internet Tablet. This device has a large, bright 4.8-inch (12cm), high-definition (HD) screen. The Archos 5 is Wi-Fi enabled so viewers can connect to the Internet to watch YouTube videos and stream movies. The device also offers Internet radio. When it is plugged into the digital video recorder (DVR) dock, the tablet is capable of recording video files.

One of the strengths of portable media players like the Archos 5 is that they will play many types of audio and visual files, including those that are exclusive to Apple and Microsoft operating systems. However, critics say that this flexibility is also a drawback. Because it lacks the sophisticated Apple or Microsoft operating systems, the "custom OS [is] too glitchy for comfort,"[60] says reviewer Jose Fermoso, and it makes the player difficult to operate under some circumstances. However, glitches in system software are fixable, and companies like Archos hope to profit from the trend toward portable players that deliver media on demand on large HD screens.

Projecting Images

The latest developments in watching movies and videos are in handheld projectors, or pico projectors. These small devices might someday make computers, and even televisions, obsolete.

The Microvision Show WX, unveiled at the Macworld Conference & Expo in January 2009, is one of the smallest of the small projectors. The Show, which is not much bigger than an iPhone, can be connected to an iPod, smartphone, or portable media player to project a widescreen, DVD-quality image on a wall. The picture ranges in size from 12 inches to 100 inches (30cm to 254cm) across. The battery in the projector holds about a two-and-a-half-hour charge, which allows users to watch most full-length films without recharging. According to Microvision's chief executive officer, Alexander Tokman,

> while mobile multimedia . . . services are on the rise . . . providers view tiny cell phone displays as a barrier to stronger consumer adoption of their products and services. With Microvision's projector, you could view and share everything ranging from YouTube videos, MSN newscasts, and Google search results to PowerPoint presentations, feature-length films, and family photos in a large, full-color, high-resolution format.[61]

While the five-hundred-dollar Show performs amazing feats, it requires a separate device, such as a digital media player or smartphone, to operate. To eliminate the need for extra hardware, Logic Wireless launched the Bolt in

Wireless show projectors such as Microvision's Show WX, displayed here, project images from devices like the iPhone onto a larger screen.

January 2009. This device is a convergent smartphone with a built-in pico projector that can cast images 36 to 64 inches (91cm to 163cm) in size. The Bolt can also play a two-hour movie, as well as share business presentations and cell-phone pictures.

Media Hookups

While pico projectors are portable, their images might appear faded unless users are in a very dark room. The projectors are also relatively expensive. For some, the answer to media adaptability lies in digital media receivers, also called HD media players. These devices contain hard drives that play audio, video, and photo files through home entertainment centers.

Apple led the way in the development of media receivers, launching Apple TV in January 2007. This small, simple, stylish box allows users to connect their broadband Internet to their widescreen, high-definition TV (HDTV). With Apple TV users can download and play digital content, including movies, videos, and TV shows purchased from the iTunes Store. iPod users can plug their players into the receiver and listen to their audio files on their home stereo systems. They can also view content from podcasts or Web sites, such as YouTube and Flickr.

Critics complain about Apple TV because users of the $229 receiver can only access feature films provided by the iTunes Store. Movies from Netflix, one of the most popular DVD rental companies, cannot be watched on Apple TV. Netflix responded by launching the Roku, a small set-top box that allows the company's customers to stream the latest films directly onto their TVs. The Roku cannot download films and does not play videos or other digital files. However, for those who have Netflix accounts, the Roku provides instant access to about twelve thousand movies at no extra charge.

BITS & BYTES

2 Billion

Number of apps downloaded from the iTunes Store between July 2008 and November 2009

Despite the challenges from Netflix and others, in 2009 Apple reported record three-month, or quarterly sales. Between July and September the company's profits increased 47 percent on nearly $10 billion in revenue. Over 7.4 million people bought iPhones, an increase of 7 percent, and more than 3 million bought Apple computers, up 17 percent. In addition the company sold 10.2 million iPods. These numbers show that Apple remained a successful industry leader in digital media for nearly eight years, a remarkable feat in the highly competitive electronics industry.

The "I Am Rich" iPhone App

Apple offers more than eighty-five thousand iPhone apps on the iTunes App Store. Most are free but some cost a few dollars. Some apps have been controversial and banned by Apple. In August 2008 the company pulled one app from its store because it cost a ridiculous amount of money and had no function. The "I Am Rich" app sold for a thousand dollars. Designed by German software developer Armin Heinrich, the app displayed a glowing red ruby image on the screen. According to Heinrich's description on the iTunes Store, "the red icon on your iPhone or iPod touch always reminds you (and others when you show it to them) that you were rich enough to afford this. It's a work of art with no hidden function at all." Eight people purchased the useless application, and Apple received nearly three hundred dollars for each one it sold. However, one day after the app went on sale, Apple banned it from the iTunes Store in response to someone who accidentally downloaded the app, thinking it was a joke.

Quoted in Lilly Peel, "Apple Sees Red over iPhone 'I Am Rich' Ruby," TimesOnline, August 8, 2008, http://business.timesonline.co.uk/tol/business/industry_sectors/technology/article4481084.ece.

Future Developments

As long as the marketplace demands it, engineers will continue to invent new and exciting ways to provide digital media through a variety of devices. While it is difficult to predict the future, there is a small army of observers who analyze subtle moves in the digital media market in hopes of divining the next big breakthrough. Because of its previous record for introducing groundbreaking devices, Apple is the most closely watched company. For example, Web sites such as Apple Insider and Mac Rumors keep track of Apple's latest patents, which give the company exclusive rights to make or sell an invention.

In late 2009 Apple Insider reported that Apple patented a software syncing system. This would allow users to share music, video, word, and other files from whatever Apple product they are using. For example, someone using a Mac computer could access files stored on an iPhone, iPod, or Apple TV. The system could share Safari bookmarks, iTunes content, Time Machine backups, keynote presentations, and saved video game files.

Apple is also said to be considering the addition of radio-frequency identification (RFID) capabilities to the iPhone and Touch. If so, other companies will likely follow. RFID tags are tiny electronic information devices, much like bar codes. They are used by shipping companies and retailers to track packages. Libraries use the tags to track books; farmers use them to identify animals in herds; and the U.S. Army attaches RFIDs to people so they can be found if killed, wounded, or captured. If RFID tags were incorporated into phones, the devices could enable what are called "touchless" technologies to perform a variety of tasks. For example, people will be able to pay for goods at a store checkout lane using their smartphones and media players, like credit cards. They could also pass through tollbooths on the highway without slowing down, purchase items from vending machines, or even use their media players in place of ignition keys in specially equipped cars.

Thomas Edison uses the phonograph, an early recording device, in the late nineteenth century. Recording technology has advanced greatly since then.

Supercharged Media Players

In 2009 Microsoft's chief executive officer, Steve Ballmer, said that Microsoft was "going to keep going with Zune . . . [but] I won't say full steam ahead."[62] This was interpreted by industry analysts to mean that Microsoft had given up trying to compete with the iPod. Whatever the fate of Zune, engineers throughout the world are doubtlessly working to create the next generation of supercharged media players to compete with iPods. And they will probably make the current devices look as old fashioned as giant desktop monitors from the 1980s. Some predict MP3 players will be encased in wristwatches, worn on the finger like rings, or worn on the wrist in the form of multimedia bracelets. These stylish devices would function with a detached multitouch track pad and wireless earbuds.

When Thomas Edison invented the phonograph in 1877, no one could have imagined the day when the human voice and musical instruments would move through the air as computer code on Wi-Fi networks. And even the most-advanced thinkers of today cannot dream of what form digital media players will take in the twenty-second century. They might be implanted under the skin and operated with thought waves. Whatever the future holds, one thing is certain. Technology will continue to advance, and digital players will keep on changing to fit the needs, demands, and creative impulses of consumers.

NOTES

Introduction:
A Rocking Revolution

1. Quoted in Jeffrey S. Young and William L. Simon, *iCon*, Hoboken, NJ: Wiley, 2005, p. 285.
2. Quoted in Young and Simon, *iCon*, p. 275.
3. Quoted in Steven Levy, "The iPod Revolution," *Los Angeles Times*, October 22, 2006, www.latimes.com/news/printedition/opinion/la-op-levy22oct22,0,3780790.story.
4. Steven Levy, *The Perfect Thing*, New York: Simon & Schuster, 2006, pp. 2–3.
5. Trey Treviño, "iPods Get in the Way of Social Interaction," *Daily Campus*, September 23, 2009, www.smudailycampus.com/2.6638/ipods-get-in-the-way-of-social-interaction-1.959958.

Chapter 1:
The Digital
Media Explosion

6. J. D. Bartlett, "Rock 101: Home Taping Is Killing Music," WNEW.com, February 12, 2009, www.wnew.com/2009/02/rock-101-home-taping-is-killing-music.html.

7. Stephen Koepp and Barbara Kraft, "The Bright New Sound of Music," *Time*, July 1, 1985, www.time.com/time/magazine/article/0,9171,959555,00.html.
8. Quoted in Steve Knopper, *Appetite for Self-Destruction*, New York: Free Press, 2009, p. 77.
9. Quoted in Knopper, *Appetite for Self-Destruction*, p. 79.
10. Chris O'Malley, "A New Spin," *Time*, August 24, 1998, www.time.com/time/magazine/article/0,9171,988955,00.html.
11. Quoted in Malley, "A New Spin."
12. Quoted in Levy, *Perfect Thing*, p. 147.
13. Quoted in Greg Kot, *Ripped*, New York: Scribner, 2009, pp. 27–28.
14. Quoted in Kot, *Ripped*, p. 31.
15. Quoted in Kot, *Ripped*, p. 35.

Chapter 2:
Portable Digital Players

16. Bill Kincaid, "The True Story of SoundJam," Panic, www.panic.com/extras/audionstory/popup-sjstory.html.
17. Kincaid, "The True Story of SoundJam."

18. Kincaid, "The True Story of SoundJam."
19. Levy, *Perfect Thing*, p. 28.
20. Quoted in Levy, *Perfect Thing*, p. 29.
21. Quoted in Young and Simon, *iCon*, p. 275.
22. Quoted in Levy, *Perfect Thing*, p. 31.
23. Quoted in Leander Kahney, "Inside Look at Birth of the iPod," *Wired*, July 21, 2004, www.wired.com/gadgets/mac/news/2004/07/64286.
24. Quoted in Kahney, "Inside Look at Birth of the iPod."
25. Quoted in Kahney, "Inside Look at Birth of the iPod."
26. Quoted in Erik Sherman, "Inside the Apple iPod Design Triumph," *Electronics Design Chain*, Summer 2002, www.designchain.com/coverstory.asp?issue=summer02.
27. Quoted in Sherman, "Inside the Apple iPod Design Triumph."
28. Quoted in Michael Bull, *Sound Moves: iPod Culture and Urban Experience*, London: Routeledge, 2007, p. 3.
29. Quoted in Brad King and Farhad Manjoo, "Apple's 'Breakthrough' iPod," *Wired*, October 23, 2001, www.wired.com/gadgets/miscellaneous/news/2001/10/47805.
30. Quoted in City of Sound, "The Rise and Rise of the Shuffle Mode," City of Sound, January 12, 2005, www.cityofsound.com/blog/2005/01/the_rise_and_ri.html.
31. Quoted in Bull, *Sound Moves*, p. 47.
32. Quoted in Conrad Quilty-Harper, "Gates Praises iPod, Labels Zune a 'Modest' Competitor," Engadget, November 18, 2006, www.engadget.com/2006/11/18/gates-praises-ipod-labels-zune-a-modest-competitor.
33. David Pogue, "Tuning in a Zippier Zune," *New York Times*, September 16, 2009, www.nytimes.com/2009/09/17/technology/personaltech/17pogue.html?pagewanted=all.
34. Levy, *Perfect Thing*, p. 255.

Chapter 3: File-Sharing Frenzy

35. Quoted in Attack of the iZombies, "iPods Are Our Foes," Attack of the iZombies, www.ocf.berkeley.edu/~krystles/NegativeEffects.html.
36. Nicholas Carr, *The Big Switch: Rewiring the World from Edison to Google*, New York: Norton, 2008, p. 20.
37. Quoted in Kot, *Ripped*, p. 42.
38. Quoted in Kot, *Ripped*, p. 43.
39. Quoted in Eric Olsen, "Just Keep Looking over Your Shoulder, We Will Get You," Blogcritics.org, June 27, 2003, http://blogcritics.org/scitech/article/just-keep-looking-over-your-shoulder.
40. Quoted in Lorena Mongelli, "Music Pirate: N.Y. Girl, 12, Sued for Web Songs Theft," *New York Post*, September 9, 2003, www.nypost.com/p/news/music_pirate_girl_sued_for_web_songs_YaK2lL6oI-6exVKpDU0jeGN.

41. Quoted in Mongelli, "Music Pirate."
42. Quoted in Jeff Goodell, "Steve Jobs: The Rolling Stone Interview," *Rolling Stone*, December 3, 2003, www.rollingstone.com/news/story/5939600/steve_jobs_the_rolling_stone_interview/3.
43. Quoted in MacDailyNews, "Apple's iTunes Music Store Sells 100 Millionth Song," MacDailyNews, July 12, 2004, www.macdailynews.com/index.php/weblog/comments/3455.
44. Quoted in Levy, *Perfect Thing*, p. 167.
45. ReverbNation, "About ReverbNation," ReverbNation, www.reverbnation.com/main/about.
46. David Pogue, "Tuning in a Zippier Zune."
47. Steve Jobs, "Thoughts on Music," www.apple.com, February 6, 2007, www.apple.com/hotnews/thoughtsonmusic.
48. Quoted in Ben Sisario, "Music Sales Fell in 2008, but Climbed on the Web," *New York Times*, December 31, 2008, www.nytimes.com/2009/01/01/arts/music/01indu.html.

Chapter 4:
Podcasts, Vodcasts, and Audiobooks

49. Quoted in Levy, *Perfect Thing*, p. 235.
50. Quoted in Levy, *Perfect Thing*, p. 237.
51. Quoted in Levy, *Perfect Thing*, p. 239.
52. Quoted in Annalee Newitz, "Adam Curry Wants to Make You an iPod Radio Star," *Wired*, March 2005, www.wired.com/wired/archive/13.03/curry.html.
53. Quoted in *National Post*, "Doctor! I Need a Triple," *National Post*, January 30, 2006, www.canada.com/nationalpost/artslife/story.html?id=aadbdfb5-4d90-424e-b638-4c9232c69cdf&k=56529.
54. Quoted in Jefferson Graham, "Duke's Free iPods Will Go Just for Classes," *USA Today*, April 6, 2005, www.usatoday.com/money/industries/technology/2005-04-06-ipod-usat_x.htm.

Chapter 5:
The Next Generation

55. Quoted in Ryan Block, "Live from Macworld 2007: Steve Jobs Keynote," Engadget, January 9, 2007, www.engadget.com/2007/01/09/live-from-macworld-2007-steve-jobs-keynote.
56. David Pogue "Apple Fills in Some Gaps with Latest iPhone," *New York Times*, June 18, 2009, www.nytimes.com/2009/06/18/technology/personaltech/18pogue.html.
57. David Pogue, "New Models from Motorola, HTC and BlackBerry," *New York Times*, October 28, 2009, www.nytimes.com/2009/10/29/technology/personaltech/29pogue.html.

58. Quoted in Wailin Wong, "Verizon Ads Touting Motorola's 'iPhone Killer,'" *Chicago Tribune*, October 19, 2009.

59. Brian X. Chen, "Android Army Pumped for All-Out Attack on iPhone," *Wired*, October 30, 2009, www.wired.com/gadgetlab/2009/10/phones.

60. Jose Fermoso, "Archos 5 Internet Tablet," *Wired*, September 26, 2008, www.wired.com/reviews/product/archos_5_internet_tablet.

61. Quoted in Elena Malykhina, "Microvision to Unwrap Small Mobile Projector at CES," *Information Week*, January 2, 2008, www.informationweek.com/news/mobility/showArticle.jhtml?articleID=205207074.

62. Quoted in Peter Kafka, "Live from New York: Microsoft CEO Steve Ballmer," All Things Digital, March 19, 2009, http://mediamemo.allthingsd.com/20090319/live-from-new-york-microsoft-ceo-steve-ballmer.

GLOSSARY

binary code: A system of representing text, sounds, pictures, or computer processor instructions using binary numbers, or the digits zero and one. Binary code is the language of all computerized devices.

byte: A unit of computer memory equal to a single character, such as a letter or number.

copyright: A law that gives artists, publishers, and record companies the right to control the use and reproduction of original works.

file sharing: The practice of distributing or providing access to digitally stored information, such as songs, videos, or e-books.

gigabyte: A unit of computer memory used to describe the size of a computer hard drive.

MP3: A coding and compression technology that reduces the size of a CD music file to one-twelfth of its original size; technically referred to as MPEG-1 Audio Layer 3.

peer-to-peer (P2P): A computer network set up so anonymous users can share music, video, and other files with one another over the Internet.

Really Simple Syndication (RSS): A system that delivers digital feeds of audio, video, or other files to subscribers whenever they are connected to the Internet.

software: Computer programs that help users perform tasks or serve as central operating systems for electronic devices.

sync: Short for synchronize, to make electronics or computer programs work together in unison.

FOR MORE INFORMATION

Books

Guy Hart-Davis, *Do It-Yourself iPod Projects: 24 Cool Things You Didn't Know You Could Do!* New York: McGraw-Hill, 2007. This book demonstrates how to use the iPod to play videos on a TV, record voices, read e-mail and e-books, and more.

Michael W. Geoghegan, *Podcast Solutions: The Complete Guide to Audio and Video Podcasting.* Berkeley, CA: Friends of Ed, 2007. This book explains podcasting, vodcasting, and issues related to the popular phenomenon.

Scott Gillam, *Steve Jobs: Apple & iPod Wizard.* This is a biography about the visionary founder of Apple Inc. and his role in designing the world's most popular digital media player.

Jesse David Hollington, *iPod & iTunes: Portable Genius.* Indianapolis, IN: Wiley 2009. This book offers a comprehensive look at the iPod and its features and functions.

Greg Kot, *Ripped.* New York: Scribner, 2009. This book describes how a new generation of computer users revolutionized the music industry through file sharing and digital media players.

Web Sites

Apple (www.apple.com). This is the corporate Web site of Apple, Inc. It features iTunes, iPods, iPhones, Macintosh computers, and news about all things concerning Apple products and software.

How Stuff Works: iPods (http:// electronics.howstuffworks.com/ ipod.htm). This Web site offers explanations of how iPods work, written in nontechnical language. It includes a library of articles about iPods, including how different models work.

Wired Science (www.pbs.org/kcet/ wiredscience). This site features stories and videos that examine popular ideas about modern technology.

Zune (www.zune.net). This Microsoft site features the latest Zune models, the Zune Marketplace, and more.

INDEX

PICTURE CREDITS

ABOUT THE AUTHOR

Stuart A. Kallen is the author of more than 250 nonfiction books for children and young adults. He has written on topics ranging from the theory of relativity to the history of rock and roll. Kallen has also written award-winning children's videos and television scripts. In his spare time, he is a singer/songwriter/guitarist in San Diego, California.